Domestic Violence

Independence Educational Publishers

First published by Independence Educational Publishers

The Studio, High Green

Great Shelford

Cambridge CB22 5EG

England

© Independence 2016

Photocopy licence

The material in this book is protected by copyright. However, the
purchaser is free to make multiple copies of particular articles for instructional
purposes for immediate use within the purchasing institution.

Making copies of the entire book is not permitted.

ISBN-13: 978 1 86168 737 1

Printed in Great Britain
Zenith Print Group

Contents

Introduction

Domestic Violence is Volume 296 in the **ISSUES** series. The aim of the series is to offer current, diverse information about important issues in our world, from a UK perspective.

ABOUT DOMESTIC VIOLENCE

In 2015, two women in England and Wales were killed every week as a result of domestic violence. However, it's not just women who suffer from partner violence; 12% of men say that they have been a victim of domestic abuse since the age of 16. This book explores the many myths and facts that surround perceptions of domestic violence. It also looks at different types of abuse, worldwide statistics and the protection offered by the law. In the final chapter, it considers the prevention of domestic violence, including perpetrator programmes, refuges and helplines.

OUR SOURCES

Titles in the **ISSUES** series are designed to function as educational resource books, providing a balanced overview of a specific subject.

The information in our books is comprised of facts, articles and opinions from many different sources, including:

⇨ Newspaper reports and opinion pieces

⇨ Website factsheets

⇨ Magazine and journal articles

⇨ Statistics and surveys

⇨ Government reports

⇨ Literature from special interest groups.

A NOTE ON CRITICAL EVALUATION

Because the information reprinted here is from a number of different sources, readers should bear in mind the origin of the text and whether the source is likely to have a particular bias when presenting information (or when conducting their research). It is hoped that, as you read about the many aspects of the issues explored in this book, you will critically evaluate the information presented.

It is important that you decide whether you are being presented with facts or opinions. Does the writer give a biased or unbiased report? If an opinion is being expressed, do you agree with the writer? Is there potential bias to the 'facts' or statistics behind an article?

ASSIGNMENTS

In the back of this book, you will find a selection of assignments designed to help you engage with the articles you have been reading and to explore your own opinions. Some tasks will take longer than others and there is a mixture of design, writing and research-based activities that you can complete alone or in a group.

FURTHER RESEARCH

At the end of each article we have listed its source and a website that you can visit if you would like to conduct your own research. Please remember to critically evaluate any sources that you consult and consider whether the information you are viewing is accurate and unbiased.

Useful weblinks

blogs.citizensadvice.org

www.theconversation.com

www.gov.uk

www.thehotline.org

www.huffingtonpost.co.uk

www.ibtimes.co.uk

kjonnsforskning.no/en

www.lancaster.ac.uk

www.lbbd.gov.uk

www.liveboldandbloom.com

www.mankindnews.wordpress.com

www.pet-owners.co.uk

www.pressassociation.com

www.refuge.org.uk

www.safelives.org.uk

www.tees.ac.uk

www.telegraph.co.uk

toysoldier.wordpress.com

www.thetrainingeffect.co.uk

www.west-midlands.police.uk

www.wgn.org.uk

www.who.int

Domestic violence – the facts

General

⇨ Two women are killed every week in England and Wales by a current or former partner (Office of National Statistics, 2015) – one woman killed every three days.

⇨ One in four women in England and Wales will experience domestic violence in their lifetimes and 8% will suffer domestic violence in any given year (Crime Survey of England and Wales, 2013/14).

⇨ Globally, one in three women will experience violence at the hands of a male partner (State of the World's Fathers Report, MenCare, 2015).

⇨ Domestic violence has a higher rate of repeat victimisation than any other crime (Home Office, July 2002).

⇨ Every minute police in the UK receive a domestic assistance call – yet only 35% of domestic violence incidents are reported to the police (Stanko, 2000 and Home Office, 2002).

⇨ The 2001/02 British Crime Survey (BCS) found that there were an estimated 635,000 incidents of domestic violence in England and Wales. 81% of the victims were women and 19% were men. Domestic violence incidents also made up nearly 22% of all violent incidents reported by participants in the BCS (Home Office, July 2002).

⇨ On average, a woman is assaulted 35 times before her first call to the police (Jaffe, 1982).

Children

⇨ 25% of children in the UK have been exposed to domestic abuse (Radford et al. NSPCC, 2011).

⇨ In 90% of domestic violence incidents in family households, children were in the same or the next room (Hughes, 1992).

⇨ 62% of children in households where domestic violence is happening are also directly harmed (SafeLives, 2015).

Health

⇨ 30% of domestic violence either starts or will intensify during pregnancy (Department of Health report, October 2004).

⇨ Foetal morbidity from violence is more prevalent than gestational diabetes or pre-eclampsia (Friend, 1998).

Cost to society

⇨ In November 2009, Sylvia Walby of the University of Leeds estimated the total costs of domestic violence to be £15.7 billion a year. This is broken down as follows:

• The costs to services (Criminal Justice System, health, social services, housing, civil legal) amount to £3.8 billion per year.

• The loss to the economy – where women take time off work due to injuries – is £1.9 billion per year.

• Domestic violence also leads to pain and suffering that is not counted in the cost of services. The human and emotional costs of domestic violence amount to almost £10 billion per year.

⇨ The above information is reprinted with kind permission from Refuge. Please visit www.refuge.org.uk for further information.

© Refuge 2016

Male victims of domestic violence and partner abuse, key facts from the ManKind Initiative

• 12.2% of men state they have been a victim of domestic abuse since they were 16. For every three victims of domestic abuse, two will be female and one will be male.

• 4% of men and 8.2% of women were estimated to have experienced domestic abuse in 2014/15, equivalent to an estimated 600,000 male victims and 1.3 million female victims.

• Partner abuse (non-sexual) was the most commonly experienced type of intimate violence among both men (2.4%) and women (5.8%) in 2014/15 closely followed by stalking (2.4% and 4.9% respectively).

• Male victims (29%) are over twice as likely than women (12%) to not tell anyone about the partner abuse they are suffering from. Only 10% of male victims will tell the police (26% women), only 23% will tell a person in an official position (43% women) and only 11% (23% women) will tell a health professional.

Source: Male victims of domestic violence and partner abuse, 30 key facts, March 2016. ManKind Initiative. For further statistics about male victims of domestic violence, please visit www.mankind.org.uk.

Domestic violence is now out in the open but the figures show just how endemic it is

An article from The Conversation.

THE CONVERSATION

By Anne Lazenbatt, NSPCC Reader in Childhood Studies, Queen's University Belfast and John Devaney, Senior Lecturer, Queen's University Belfast

Domestic violence is physically, emotionally, psychologically and socially devastating to women and can have similarly devastating effects on their infants and children. The Home Office highlights that while domestic violence can be directed at men by women and can happen in same-sex relationships, the unequivocal majority of domestic abuse (more than 77%) is committed by men against women. In the UK, one in four women experiences domestic violence and this violence accounts for almost a quarter of all crime.

This violence can take many forms including physical (hitting, kicking, restraining), sexual (including assault, coercion, female genital mutilation), psychological (verbal bullying, undermining, social isolation) and financial (withholding money or demanding unrealistic expectations with the household budget). The human cost to victims and families can be enormous, including the breakdown in relationships and families, and a reduction in life opportunities for individuals and children.

A view from Northern Ireland

We've been researching the devastating effects of domestic violence on women and children in Northern Ireland for the past ten years and what we've found gives a good picture of how and where violence happens. Like the UK figure, one in four women in Northern Ireland will likely experience domestic violence at some point in their lives, and some 11,000 children live with domestic violence.

This can have immediate and lifelong traumatic effects to health and well-being. Statistics from the Police Service of Northern Ireland (PSNI) show that there were more than 27,500 incidents of domestically motivated violence in 2013–14 – this accounts for a third of all reported crimes and corresponds to a domestic incident every 19 minutes of every day of the year.

The British Crime Survey suggests that women are at greater risk of repeat victimisation and serious injury; 89% of those suffering four or more incidents are women. However, the problem appears slightly greater in Northern Ireland, where the NI Crime Survey revealed that almost half (49%) of women with repeat victimisation experienced domestic violence from a perpetrator on more than one occasion, and that a quarter (27%) were victimised on four or more occasions. For 56% of this group the violence and abuse started around the time of pregnancy and delivery of a baby.

We know that domestic violence has serious health consequences and is a common cause of physical injury; depression and alcohol/drug misuse; self-harm and suicide and has serious effects in pregnancy and older age. In its most extreme form, domestic violence kills women – seven women were killed in Northern Ireland in 2013.

Only around a quarter of women ever report their worst assault to the police, and, on average, a victim is assaulted 35 times before reporting the incident or seeking support. It has also been estimated that only 29% of domestic violence incidents are reported and in reality, we do not know the full extent of the problem. In 2013, Women's Aid (NI) provided refuge to 1,077 women and 854 children, with 2,938 women

accessing their floating support service, which enables women to access support while remaining in their own homes and communities.

Vulnerable groups

Women are vulnerable to violence at certain times of their life. Pregnancy is seen as a period of significant risk and it is well-recognised that domestic violence is more likely to begin or escalate during this time. Of women who suffer abuse, 35% experience an increase during pregnancy and the post-natal period leading to increased rates of depression and anxiety and substance misuse.

Older women aged over 50 who are victims of domestic violence are also a vulnerable group and may suffer silently because the problem is often ignored. These older women face serious barriers to accessing support and are offered few appropriate services when they manage to enter the service system. Psychological abuse has the strongest impact on older women's lives by destroying their self-confidence, self-efficacy and coping abilities.

Children and adolescents are extremely vulnerable to domestic violence. Within the UK it is estimated that up to one million children have been exposed to domestic violence, yet, in spite of these stark statistics, there has until recently been a systemic failure by public agencies to appreciate that the presence of domestic violence should be an indicator of the importance of assessing children's need for support and protection if they live in the same household as the victim.

Alarmingly, between 55% and 90% of domestic violence occurs when children and young people are present or nearby, and this violence has serious, negative consequences on their immediate and lifelong health and well-being.

Studies show that these children experience serious traumatic effects and high levels of depression and anxiety and low self-esteem; exhibit behavioural problems and developmental delay. Domestic violence and child abuse and neglect are inter-connected. At its worst, domestic violence and/or child abuse is associated with mortality in children under five years, and infants in their first year of life are particularly vulnerable.

Internationally, domestic violence is a serious criminal, human rights and public safety problem with serious consequences for families and society, but it is only relatively recently that the issue has been recognised as something not kept private, to remain between people in their own homes. There is no doubt that this violence constitutes a significant public health issue and children growing up with violence can only be detrimental to society as a whole. The figures above show it's clear that we need new ways to tackle what is an endemic problem.

19 January 2015

⇨ The above information is reprinted with kind permission from *The Conversation*. Please visit www.theconversation.com for further information.

Types of domestic abuse

There are many kinds of domestic abuse. Some of them are outlined here. Please be aware of what domestic abuse is and be sure you could recognise it in your partner's behaviour, your own behaviour or the behaviour of people you know.

Physical abuse includes:

⇨ Hitting you

⇨ Biting you

⇨ Strangling you

⇨ Kicking you.

Sexual abuse:

⇨ Forcing you to have sex

⇨ Touching you

⇨ Making you do things you don't want to

⇨ Not allowing you to take contraception

⇨ Forcing you to look at or watch graphic materials.

Emotional or psychological abuse:

⇨ Constantly checking up on you by phone or text

⇨ Calling you names

⇨ Putting you down

⇨ Humiliating you

⇨ Making you feel guilty or bad about yourself

⇨ Threatening to take your children away

⇨ Using your children to relay messages.

Financial abuse:

⇨ Taking your money

⇨ Taking your benefits

⇨ Monitoring what you spend.

Social abuse:

⇨ Stopping you from seeing your friends or family

⇨ Stopping you from contacting your friends or family

⇨ Checking your phone or text messages.

Forced marriage:

⇨ One or both parties not wishing to be married

⇨ Distinct from arranged marriage, where both parties have to agree to the arrangement of their marriage.

Honour-based violence:

⇨ Extreme punishments or harassment for breaking a strict 'moral code'

⇨ Fear of the above

⇨ Punishment or harassment for supporting a victim of 'honour' based violence.

Female genital mutilation

(sometimes mistakenly called female circumcision.)

May be seen by:

⇨ Family belongs to a community in which female genital mutilation is practised making preparations for the child to take a holiday, arranging vaccinations or planning absence from school

⇨ Prolonged absence from school with noticeable behaviour change on return, or

⇨ Long periods away from classes or other normal activities, possibly with bladder or menstrual problems.

Socially isolating abuse:

⇨ Not letting you go out or go out on your own

⇨ Stopping you from seeing friends or family

⇨ Stopping you from working

⇨ Stopping you from having enough money to go out

⇨ Stopping you from learning English.

⇨ The above information is reprinted with kind permission from the London Borough of Barking & Dagenham. Please visit www.lbbd.gov.uk for further information.

Myths vs facts

Below, the Women and Girls Network has gathered some of the most common myths about violence against women, along with the facts.

MYTH: Violence is when someone is physically injured

FACT: Violence against women extends beyond just the physical. Acts such as calling a woman names, constantly criticising her, forcing her to dress in a certain way, not allowing her to use contraception, forcing her to have abortions, isolating her from family and friends, pressurising her to get married are all forms of violence against women. The impact of these actions are devastating and although they do not necessarily leave physical scars, the emotional and psychological trauma can take years to heal.

MYTH: Some religions state that violence against women and girls is OK

FACT: No religion says it is OK to abuse women and girls. However, some abusers try to use their own interpretation of their religion as a justification for violence. This interpretation may be supported by some members of the wider community but this does not mean that what they believe should be seen as more authentic or valid than other more progressive views. Domestic violence is a crime and is against the law and religion does not change that.

MYTH: Rape is horrific – but it's not very common

FACT: 3.7 million women in England and Wales have been sexually assaulted at some point since the age of 16. Around 10,000 women are sexually assaulted, and 2,000 women are raped, every week. 34% of all rapes recorded by the police are committed against children under 16 years of age. Given how common rape is, the level of reporting to the police is very low. Surveys carried out all over the world show that between 50% to over 90% of women do not report rape to the police.

MYTH: Rape and sexual assault usually happen late at night on quiet roads and in parks

FACT: Rape and sexual assault happen in different places. Women and girls report being raped and assaulted in their own homes, at work, at school, in clubs and bars, in the homes of the rapist and sometimes they do not know where they were assaulted. Regardless of where a woman or a girl is assaulted she is still entitled to protection, support and care if she chooses to report to the police.

MYTH: Women and girls are most likely to be raped by a stranger

FACT: The reality is that women and girls are more likely to be raped by someone they know. This could be a boyfriend, husband, friend, work colleague, classmate, acquaintance or a member of their family. 97% of women who contacted Rape Crisis said they knew the person who raped them. 43% of girls questioned in a national survey said the person responsible for an unwanted sexual experience was a boy they knew or were friends with.

MYTH: Young women who wear revealing clothes are more likely to be raped

FACT: Rapists do not target women and girls just because of the way they look. From children of a few months old, to women in their 90s, women of all ages and appearances are raped. Blaming the way a woman or a girl dresses is a way of justifying the behaviour of rapists. Whether a woman is wearing a pair of jeans, a skirt, hijab, school uniform or a salwar kameez has nothing to do with why she was raped. Rape is an act of dominance, control and power.

MYTH: If a girl accepts drink, drugs, gifts or money from a boy, then of course he would expect her to have sex with him and his friends

FACT: This is a form of exploitation and usually the people supplying alcohol, money and gifts have the power in this relationship and will use this to their advantage. Girls who are exploited are likely to be coming from a position of vulnerability such as previous abuse, family breakdown, low self-esteem and disengaging from school and are unlikely to be truly consenting to this type of sexual activity.

MYTH: If a girl does not say 'no' to sex, it means she has consented

FACT: Just because a girl/woman does not say no, this does not mean she has consented to sex. Depending on the situation, it is not always possible to say no and even if she does say no, the boy/man she is with may not respect her decision and might continue to pressure her into having sex. There are other ways that a boy/man is able to recognise a girl/woman does not want to have sex such as the fact she is crying, she looks uncomfortable or scared or that she is completely silent and still. In a safe and healthy situation it is possible for them to talk about whether they are both ready to have sex. However, in a situation that is being controlled and dominated by the boy/man, this type of discussion is unlikely to take place. If a boy/man has sex with a girl who has not actively consented, he is committing an act of rape for which he can be prosecuted.

MYTH: It is common for women and girls to lie about being raped

FACT: The level of false reporting is very low. Research suggests that it is about 2% and in fact other crimes such as burglary have a higher rate of false reporting because of insurance claims. The reality is that women and girls are reluctant to report rape because they are afraid they will not be believed and feel ashamed about what has happened to them.

MYTH: Women scream and shout when they are being raped

FACT: Responses to rape and sexual assault vary. Some women may scream and physically 'fight back' whilst others are not able to do so. This is because some women 'freeze' due to fear, if there are several perpetrators she may be too scared to 'resist' or if she is drunk her ability to 'fight back' will be affected by alcohol. It is easy to assume how a woman should react when she is being raped. However, the reality for victims is that they are trying to survive a frightening and traumatic ordeal and will do whatever they believe will ensure that they won't be subjected to further harm and abuse.

MYTH: Child sexual abuse is not a widespread problem

FACT: 59% of young women suffered some form of sexual abuse (including being made to look at pornography) before they were 18.

MYTH: Most child abusers do it in a moment of madness/weakness and regret it, so they never do it again

FACT: Men who sexually abuse children can average as many as 73 victims before they are caught. Abuse takes place over an average of eight years. A sample of 561 offenders completed a total of 291,737 acts with a total of 195,407 victims (only 3% of these offences were detected).

MYTH: Only certain types of men abuse children

FACT: There is no 'type' of man who is an abuser – they come from every class, professional, racial and religious background. They are, however, mostly married men.

MYTH: Domestic violence is not a serious and widespread problem

FACT: Unfortunately, domestic violence is an everyday occurrence affecting thousands of women and their children. More than one in four women in England and Wales (4.8 million) since the age of 16 have experienced at least one incident of domestic abuse.

Every year one million women experience at least one incident of domestic abuse – nearly 20,000 women a week. The police receive a call every minute asking for help in relation to domestic violence. In the UK, two women a week are murdered by their partner or ex-partner and 500 women a year commit suicide as a result of domestic violence.

In the 15–44 age group, more women are killed globally in domestic violence attacks than in war, accidents or by cancer. Domestic violence cuts across age, ethnicity, religion, disability, sexuality and class: it is a global health problem and a human rights issue.

MYTH: Men are abused as much as women

FACT: Men can also be victims of domestic and sexual violence. However, violence against men is usually perpetrated by other men and not women. Betsy Stanko's domestic violence count found that 8% of reported assaults involved a woman assaulting a man whilst 81% of incidents involved a women being attacked by a man. Domestic and sexual violence disproportionately affects women and girls and the Scottish Crime Survey, 2002 found men are less likely to be seriously injured, repeat victims, to report feeling fearful in their own homes, and that the majority of victims are women.

MYTH: You can tell if a woman is experiencing domestic violence because she will be covered in bruises

FACT: Domestic violence is not just about physical violence and in fact includes psychological, emotional and verbal abuse. Controlling finances, keeping someone isolated, telling someone they are worthless and stupid, threats of violence, constantly checking text messages are a few examples of the acts of power and control exerted by perpetrators.

MYTH: Alcohol is one of the main causes of domestic violence

FACT: Not all men and boys who have been violent to their partners have been drinking alcohol or have an alcohol problem. Men or boys who are perpetrators of domestic violence believe that they have the right to control, dominate and hurt their partners and they hold these beliefs regardless of whether they drink alcohol or not. Alcohol is not responsible for violent and abusive behaviour, the perpetrators are.

MYTH: It is acceptable for a man/boy to video sex with his girlfriend on a mobile phone and show it to his friends or put it on the Internet

FACT: Sex is not something that has to be shared with or 'performed' for other people. Although sexually explicit behaviour is presented as being the norm, particularly through reality TV shows for example, this can promote the idea that boundaries are no longer needed and that it is acceptable to be open about very private and personal matters to people who perhaps do not care about you or are not concerned about your welfare. This is a form of exploitation and even if the girl has 'allowed' herself to be filmed, this may be because she is unable to voice her lack of consent due to low confidence, low self-esteem, peer pressure or fear and intimidation. Filming sex with anyone under 16 is a criminal offence, and the police will prosecute anyone doing this.

MYTH: When boys at school pinch girls' bottoms or touch their breasts, it is just harmless fun

FACT: This is a form of sexual bullying and harassment. It is unacceptable and against the law. If this behaviour is not challenged then it condones a form of violence against women. It sends out a message to men and boys that the bodies of women and girls are available for them to treat as they please. Figures from the academic year of 2006–2007, 3,500 pupils were suspended for sexual misconduct: sexist graffiti, name-calling, touching, sexual assault and rape. Although this kind of behaviour is illegal in the workplace, sexual harassment still happens and it is believed that one in two women experience this form of harassment.

⇨ The above information is reprinted with kind permission from the Women and Girls Network. Please visit www.wgn.org.uk for further information.

© Women and Girls Network 2016

What is gaslighting?

"You're crazy – that never happened"

"Are you sure? You tend to have a bad memory"

"It's all in your head"

Does your partner repeatedly say things like this to you? Do you often start questioning your own perception of reality, even your own sanity, within your relationship? If so, your partner may be using what mental health professionals call "gaslighting".

This term comes from the 1938 stage play *Gas Light*, in which a husband attempts to drive his wife crazy by dimming the lights (which were powered by gas) in their home, and then he denies that the light changed when his wife points it out. It is an extremely effective form of emotional abuse that causes a victim to question their own feelings, instincts and sanity, which gives the abusive partner a lot of power (and we know that abuse is about power and control). Once an abusive partner has broken down the victim's ability to trust their own perceptions, the victim is more likely to stay in the abusive relationship.

There are a variety of gaslighting techniques that an abusive partner might use:

Withholding

The abusive partner pretends not to understand or refuses to listen. Ex. "I don't want to hear this again," or "You're trying to confuse me."

Countering

The abusive partner questions the victim's memory of events, even when the victim remembers them accurately. Ex. "You're wrong, you never remember things correctly."

Blocking/Diverting

The abusive partner changes the subject and/or questions the victim's thoughts. Ex. "Is that another crazy idea you got from [friend/family member]?" or "You're imagining things."

Trivialising

The abusive partner makes the victim's needs or feelings seem unimportant. Ex. "You're going to get angry over a little thing like that?" or "You're too sensitive."

Forgetting/Denial

The abusive partner pretends to have forgotten what actually occurred or denies things like promises made to the victim. Ex. "I don't know what you're talking about," or "You're just making stuff up."

Gaslighting typically happens very gradually in a relationship; in fact, the abusive partner's actions may seem harmless at first. Over time, however, these abusive patterns continue and a victim can become confused, anxious, isolated and depressed, and they can lose all sense of what is actually happening. Then they start relying on the abusive partner more and more to define reality, which creates a very difficult situation to escape.

In order to overcome this type of abuse, it's important to start recognising the signs and eventually learn to trust yourself again. According to author and psychoanalyst Robin Stern, Ph.D., the signs of being a victim of gaslighting include:

⇨ You constantly second-guess yourself.

⇨ You ask yourself, "Am I too sensitive?" multiple times a day.

⇨ You often feel confused and even crazy.

⇨ You're always apologizing to your partner.

⇨ You can't understand why, with so many apparently good things in your life, you aren't happier.

⇨ You frequently make excuses for your partner's behaviour to friends and family.

⇨ You find yourself withholding information from friends and family so you don't have to explain or make excuses.

⇨ You know something is terribly wrong, but you can never quite express what it is, even to yourself.

⇨ You start lying to avoid the put downs and reality twists.

⇨ You have trouble making simple decisions.

⇨ You have the sense that you used to be a very different person – more confident, more fun-loving, more relaxed.

⇨ You feel hopeless and joyless.

⇨ You feel as though you can't do anything right.

⇨ You wonder if you are a "good enough" partner.

⇨ The above information is reprinted with kind permission from The National Domestic Violence Hotline. Please visit www.thehotline.org for further information.

© The National Domestic Violence Hotline 2016

My money, my life

Nearly one in five British adults say they have experienced financial abuse in an intimate relationship, according to a new ethical campaign launched by the Bank and Refuge, the national domestic violence charity.

The 'My money, my life' campaign raises awareness of the true scale of financial abuse for the first time, as it occurs within intimate relationships, where financial control, exploitation or sabotage are used to control a person's ability to acquire, use and maintain financial resources. We carried out the UK's largest study to date in this area in order to understand the prevalence of financial abuse in intimate relationships in the UK. We are campaigning for the banking industry to come together to ensure there is adequate and consistent support for the victims of financial abuse in relationships.

Key findings

⇨ One in five UK adults is a victim of financial abuse in a relationship

⇨ Half of victims experience a partner taking financial assets without permission

⇨ For women, financial abuse rarely happens in isolation – 86 per cent experience other forms of abuse

⇨ A third of financial abuse victims suffer in silence, telling no-one

⇨ Six out of ten victims of financial abuse are women

⇨ One in three people know somebody who has been financially abused.

The Co-operative Bank and Refuge, are calling for industry-wide agreement to support people who experience financial abuse in their relationships.

What is financial abuse?

Financial abuse in intimate relationships is a way of controlling a person's ability to acquire, use and maintain their own money and financial resources.

Financial abuse is a form of domestic violence. According to financial abuse expert, Nicola Jeff-Sharp from the Child and Woman Abuse Studies Unit (CWASU) at London Metropolitan University, it is best described as an example of intimate partner violence. Domestic violence involves a pattern of behaviour that one person uses to control, undermine and obtain power over another person. Domestic abuse can include physical, sexual, psychological/emotional and financial abuse. More simply, financial abuse is a current or former partner controlling someone's ability to acquire, use or maintain financial resources by preventing victims from earning or accessing their own money.

Examples include:

⇨ Stealing money from a partner

⇨ Preventing a partner from accessing their own/joint account

⇨ Damaging possessions which then have to be replaced

⇨ Insisting benefits are in their name

⇨ Putting debts in a partner's name

⇨ Stopping a partner from going to work.

This abuse can also continue post-separation.

Lifting the lid on financial abuse

One in five UK adults is a victim of financial abuse in a relationship

The 'My money, my life' campaign seeks to establish, for the first time, the true scale of financial abuse as it occurs within intimate relationships in the UK. While other forms of domestic violence are well documented, the use of money to exercise power within a relationship is not yet fully recognised. Yet the impact of this form of abuse – where financial control, exploitation or sabotage are used to control a person's ability to acquire, use and maintain financial resources – can be both devastating and long-lasting.

Our campaign launches with the publication of a new research report *Money Matters – research into the extent and nature of financial abuse in relationships in the UK*. The research report combines a study of over 4,000 adults with academic analysis and qualitative research interviews undertaken with 20 survivors of domestic abuse who had accessed Refuge's specialist services.

⇨ Financial abuse against women is more likely to start at key life stage events compared to men, for example, when moving in with a partner, getting married or having a baby.

- ⇨ Financial abuse in relationships against women also lasts for a longer period of time compared to men.

- ⇨ Women are also more likely to experience financial abuse in multiple relationships and post-separation.

- ⇨ Women experiencing financial abuse in relationships were more likely to be heterosexual and living as married, with the highest prevalence of financial abuse occurring amongst full-time working women and women working part-time.

As women are the most affected group, and the research shows they are the least likely to contact their bank for help, breaking down the barriers to enable a woman to access support from her bank is a key part of the campaign.

Overall, the report shows that while the majority of people experiencing this type of abuse are in heterosexual relationships, people in same-sex or bi-sexual relationships were more likely to be victims of financial abuse than the rest of the population. In addition, those with a disability were also more likely to be victims of financial abuse in an intimate relationship.

If you are experiencing domestic violence:

The Freephone 24-hour Domestic Violence Helpline, run in partnership by Refuge and Women's Aid, offers a 24-hour confidential helpline for women who are experiencing domestic violence. It provides emotional and practical support, including referrals to refuges and other local services: 0808 2000 247.

- ⇨ The above information is reprinted with kind permission from Refuge. Please visit www.refuge.org.uk for further information.

© Refuge 2016

30 signs of emotional abuse in a relationship

By Barrie Davenport

Nothing is more damaging to your confidence and self-esteem than being in an emotionally abusive relationship.

Unlike physical abuse which rears its ugly head in dramatic outbursts, emotional abuse can be more insidious and elusive. In some cases, neither the abuser nor the victim are fully aware it's happening.

The most obvious scenario for emotional abuse is in an intimate relationship in which a man is the abuser and the woman is the victim. However, a variety of studies show that men and women abuse each other at equal rates. In fact, emotional abuse can occur in any relationship – between parent and child, in friendships and with relatives.

So what is emotional abuse? It involves a regular pattern of verbal offence, threatening, bullying and constant criticism, as well as more subtle tactics like intimidation, shaming and manipulation. Emotional abuse is used to control and subjugate the other person, and quite often it occurs because the abuser has childhood wounds and insecurities they haven't dealt with – perhaps as a result of being abused themselves. They didn't learn healthy coping mechanisms or how to have positive, healthy relationships. Instead, they feel angry, hurt, fearful and powerless.

Male and female abusers tend to have high rates of personality disorders including borderline personality disorder, narcissistic personality disorder and antisocial personality disorder. Although emotional abuse doesn't always lead to physical abuse, physical abuse is almost always preceded and accompanied by emotional abuse.

The victim of the abuse quite often doesn't see the mistreatment as abusive. They develop coping mechanisms of denial and minimising in order to deal with the stress. But the effects of long-term emotional abuse can cause severe emotional trauma in the victim, including depression, anxiety and post-traumatic stress disorder.

If you aren't sure what constitutes this damaging behaviour, here are 30 signs of emotional abuse:

1. They humiliate you, put you down or make fun of you in front of other people.

2. They regularly demean or disregard your opinions, ideas, suggestions or needs.

3. They use sarcasm or 'teasing' to put you down or make you feel bad about yourself.

4. They accuse you of being 'too sensitive' in order to deflect their abusive remarks.

5. They try to control you and treat you like a child.

6. They correct or chastise you for your behaviour.

7. You feel like you need permission to make decisions or go out somewhere.

8. They try to control the finances and how you spend money.

9. They belittle and trivialise you, your accomplishments or your hopes and dreams.

10. They try to make you feel as though they are always right and you are wrong.

11. They give you disapproving or contemptuous looks or body language.

12. They regularly point out your flaws, mistakes or shortcomings.

13. They accuse or blame you of things you know aren't true.

14. They have an inability to laugh at themselves and can't tolerate others laughing at them.

15. They are intolerant of any seeming lack of respect.

16. They make excuses for their behaviour, try to blame others and have difficulty apologising.

17. They repeatedly cross your boundaries and ignore your requests.

18. They blame you for their problems, life difficulties or unhappiness.

19. They call you names, give you unpleasant labels or make cutting remarks under their breath.

20. They are emotionally distant or emotionally unavailable most of the time.

21. They resort to pouting or withdrawal to get attention or attain what they want.

22. They don't show you empathy or compassion.

23. They play the victim and try to deflect blame to you rather than taking personal responsibility.

24. They disengage or use neglect or abandonment to punish or frighten you.

25. They don't seem to notice or care about your feelings.

26. They view you as an extension of themselves rather than as an individual.

27. They withhold sex as a way to manipulate and control.

28. They share personal information about you with others.

29. They invalidate or deny their emotionally abusive behaviour when confronted.

30. They make subtle threats or negative remarks with the intent to frighten or control you.

The first step for those being emotionally abused is recognising it's happening. If you recognise any of the signs of emotional abuse in your relationship, you need to be honest with yourself so you can regain power over your own life, stop the abuse and begin to heal. For those who've been minimising, denying and hiding the abuse, this can be a painful and frightening first step.

The stress of emotional abuse will eventually catch up with you in the form of illness, emotional trauma, depression or anxiety. You simply can't allow it to continue, even if it means ending the relationship. A licensed counsellor who is trained in abusive relationships can help you navigate the pain and fears of leaving the relationship and work with you to rebuild your self-esteem.

Can an emotional abuser change?

It is possible if the abuser deeply desires to change and recognises his or her abusive patterns and the damage caused by them. However, the learned behaviours and feelings of entitlement and privilege are very difficult to change. The abusers tend to enjoy the power they feel from emotional abuse, and as a result, a very low percentage of abusers can turn themselves around.

According to Lundy Bancroft, author of the book *Why Does He Do That?: Inside the Minds of Angry and Controlling Men*, here are some of the changes an abuser (either man or woman) needs to make to begin recovery:

⇨ Admit fully to what they have done.

⇨ Stop making excuses and blaming others.

⇨ Make amends.

⇨ Accept responsibility and recognise that abuse is a choice.

⇨ Identify the patterns of controlling behaviour they use.

⇨ Identify the attitudes that drive their abuse.

⇨ Accept that overcoming abusiveness is a decades-long process – not declaring themselves 'cured'.

⇨ Not demanding credit for improvements they've made.

⇨ Not treating improvements as vouchers to be spent on occasional acts of abuse (ex. "I haven't done anything like this in a long time, so it's not a big deal).

⇨ Develop respectful, kind, supportive behaviours.

⇨ Carry their weight and sharing power.

⇨ Change how they respond to their partner's (or former partner's) anger and grievances.

⇨ Change how they act in heated conflicts.

⇨ Accept the consequences of their actions (including not feeling sorry for themselves about the consequences and not blaming their partner or children for them).

If the emotional abuser in your relationship isn't interested in changing, and you aren't in a position to leave the relationship immediately, here are some strategies for reclaiming your power and self-esteem for the short term:

Put your own needs first. Stop worrying about pleasing or protecting the abuser. Take care of yourself and your needs, and let the other person worry about themselves – even when they pout or try to manipulate you and control your behaviour.

Set some firm boundaries. Tell your abuser he or she may no longer yell at you, call you names, be rude to you, etc. If the bad behaviour occurs, let them know you will not tolerate it and leave the room or get in the car and drive to a friend's house.

Don't engage. If the abuser tries to pick a fight or win an argument, don't engage with anger, over-explaining yourself or apologies to try to soothe him/her. Just keep quiet and walk away.

Realise you can't 'fix' them. You can't make this person change or reason your way into their hearts and minds. They must want to change and recognise the destructive quality of their behaviour and words. You'll only feel worse about yourself and the situation by repeated 'interventions'.

You are not to blame. If you've been entrenched in an abusive relationship for a while, it can be crazy-making. You start to feel like something must be wrong with you since this other person treats you so poorly. Begin to acknowledge to yourself that it is NOT you. This is the first step towards rebuilding your self-esteem.

Seek support. Talk to trusted friends and family or a counsellor about what you are going through. Get away from the abusive person as often as possible and spend time with those who love and support you. This support system will help you feel less alone and isolated while you still contend with the abuser.

Develop an exit plan. You can't remain in an emotionally abusive relationship forever. If finances or children or some other valid reason prevents you from leaving now, develop a plan for leaving as soon as possible. Begin saving money, looking for a place to live or planning for divorce if necessary so you can feel more in control and empowered.

Emotional abuse is a form of brain-washing that slowly erodes the victim's sense of self-worth, security and trust in themselves and others. In many ways, it is more detrimental than physical abuse because it slowly disintegrates one's sense of self and personal value. It cuts to the core of your essential being, which can create lifelong psychological scars and emotional pain.

⇨ The above information is reprinted with kind permission from author Barrie Davenport. Please visit www.liveboldandbloom.com for further information.

© Barrie Davenport 2016

One in three women worldwide is a victim of partner violence

An article from The Conversation.

By Emily Lindsay Brown, Assistant Commissioning Editor, The Conversation, Jo Adetunji, Deputy Editor, The Conversation

THE CONVERSATION

A third of women worldwide have experienced physical or sexual violence at the hands of a partner, according to the first comprehensive research of its kind.

The report, published today by the London School of Hygiene and Tropical Medicine (LSHTM) and the World Health Organization (WHO), also reveals that nearly 40% of murders of women were committed by close partners.

The figures show the shocking levels of attacks on women across the globe and a catalogue of health problems caused by them.

The worst affected regions were South-East Asia where nearly 38% of women were subjected to sexual or physical violence by a close partner, followed by the Eastern Mediterranean (37%) and Africa (36.6%).

For violence committed by close partners and others, Africa was worst with 46% of women affected. Even in the European region, which reported the smallest rate, 27% of women were victims of these types of abuse.

The research is the result of a systematic review using global population data taken from two papers published in *The Lancet* and *Science* journals. Researchers used the data to look at the association between different forms of violence and its impact on women's health.

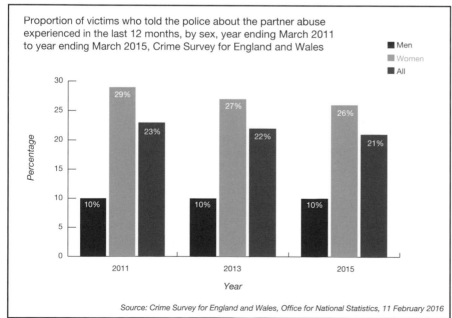

Proportion of victims who told the police about the partner abuse experienced in the last 12 months, by sex, year ending March 2011 to year ending March 2015, Crime Survey for England and Wales

Source: Crime Survey for England and Wales, Office for National Statistics, 11 February 2016

Health problems

The researchers found a huge array of health problems have their root in sexual or physical violence. Apart from immediate physical injuries, women can also encounter significant problems including mental health issues, alcohol abuse and in women who were pregnant, children with low birth weight.

Professor Charlotte Watts, from the LSHTM and a co-author of the report, said the report highlighted the high global levels of violence that happen across the globe. "We need to take this issue more seriously; it affects women in all parts of the world," said Watts.

The prevalence of the problem is likely to shock, but the wider health implications are an even greater cause for concern. Women who experience partner violence typically have less control over sex and their sexual health, including the use of condoms, according to the report. As a consequence, these women are up to 1.5 times more likely to contract HIV.

Female victims of partner abuse are also twice as likely to have an abortion. Half of abortions worldwide are thought to take place in unsafe conditions, according to the study, placing these women at even higher risk of injury or death. Victims of violence are also twice as likely to suffer depression and this figure is even higher for women who experience sexual assault from non-partners; they are more than twice as likely to become depressed and to have problems with alcohol abuse.

But the link between alcohol and violence is complicated. Women could be turning to alcohol as a coping mechanism, but their drinking could also lead to an abusive reaction from their partners, the researchers said.

Better education, employment and legal status

The researchers suggest that the numbers in the report are likely to be conservative and the true size of the problem still hidden by a lack of data and missing information. For example, a women might report health problems but not say how she was injured.

"We really need to be tackling some of the social and economic conditions that help violence to thrive," said Watts. This includes access to education and employment, economic and legal equality and social norms regarding acceptable behaviour towards women are all tied to the levels of violence that women experience.

Another solution is to provide better training for health professionals and better collection of information which can be used by policy makers. The report recommends that post-rape care needs to also be made accessible to victims through health providers within 72 hours of the attack.

Polly Neate, Chief Executive of Womens' Aid, a UK domestic violence charity, said: "Doctors need to be aware of domestic violence, able to spot it, identify it, and act on it, but too often they lack the confidence or training to take this action.

"One of the important conclusions from this work is that we need to step up action by the health sector," Watts said. She added: "Training on violence should be included in the medical training curriculum."

Dr Heidi Stöckl, lead author of *The Lancet* paper, said: "Our results underscore that women are disproportionately vulnerable to violence and murder by an intimate partner, and their needs have been neglected for far too long. Such homicides are often the ultimate outcome of a failed societal, health and criminal justice response to intimate partner violence."

But there are some examples of good work. Malaysia is currently a forerunner in the provision of care for female victims of sexual and physical assault, said Watts. "Across the country there is a national policy to make accident and emergency departments one-stop centres, where women can access a range of services, including legal and counselling services."

20 June 2013

⇨ The above information is reprinted with kind permission from *The Conversation*. Please visit www.theconversation.com for further information.

© 2010–2016, The Conversation Trust (UK)

Bullying husbands face jail under new proposals by Theresa May

Home Secretary unveils plan to criminalise 'domestic abuse' which involves no violence, in a bid to crack down on 'brutal reality' of intimidation behind closed doors.

By David Barrett, Home Affairs Correspondent

Husbands who keep their wives downtrodden could face prison under new plans set out by the Government today.

Theresa May, the Home Secretary, published proposals for a new offence of 'domestic abuse' that would criminalise men or women who bully, cause psychological harm or deny money to their partners.

The law would make the worst cases of non-violent "controlling behaviour" a jailable offence.

"The Government unveiled a 'Cinderella' law earlier this year which will see parents who starve their children of love and affection being prosecuted for 'emotional cruelty'"

Exact terms of the offence are yet to be defined, but it could involve humiliating, frightening or intimidating a partner, keeping them away from friends or family or restricting their access to money.

A 15-page consultation document issued by the Home Office said there would have to be a 'pattern' of abuse to trigger a prosecution.

It comes after the Government unveiled a 'Cinderella' law earlier this year which will see parents who starve their children of love and affection being prosecuted for 'emotional cruelty'.

Both proposed offences mark a significant incursion by the State into what have previously been regarded as private affairs.

Mrs May said she was clear that

domestic abuse was "not just about violence". "Within every community there are people living in fear of those closest to them," she said.

"The terrifying reality is that for the most part these appalling crimes happen behind closed doors. We must bring domestic abuse out into the open and send a clear message that it is wrong to put your partner or your family in fear."

Although the new domestic abuse offence is mainly designed to protect wives and girlfriends from male partners who intimidate them, it will apply equally to men being targeted by women. The Home Office said 16 per cent of men admit to being victims of domestic abuse during their lifetimes compared with 30 per cent of women, according to research.

Women's Aid, one of the groups working with the Home Office on the proposals, highlighted the case of a mother-of-two whose abusive marriage illustrated the kind of relationship that could be covered by the law.

She suffered years of psychological abuse from her husband who, she said, would "put me down", hide her possessions and "scream" at her if she came home late.

"I wasn't allowed any money for myself," she said. "He would spend £200 a week at a strip club; I had to give a comprehensive budget of everything I was spending."

In a separate case highlighted by Rachel Horman, a solicitor who specialises in domestic abuse cases, a woman was woken in the night by her husband, who had been drinking.

He ordered her to go to the garage to buy cigarettes for him, and to bring a receipt to show how much of his money she had spent.

When she returned without the receipt, he shouted obscenities at her and ordered her to get on her knees to beg his forgiveness, which she did immediately to avoid being hit.

The consultation paper acknowledged that domestic abuse was already partly covered by stalking and harassment laws, but it said a new offence might be necessary because some experts had argued that "the law is ambiguous and perpetrators are ... not being brought to justice".

A new offence would strengthen protection for people in relationships

with each other, and could also cover abuse between family members and ex-partners. The consultation, which is open for eight weeks, defines domestic abuse as "a pattern of acts of assault, threats, humiliation and intimidation or other abuse that is used to harm, punish or frighten their victim".

A Home Office spokesman said the crime would be prosecuted "along the same lines" as anti-stalking and harassment offences. Under those laws, there must have been at least two occasions when the victim was caused distress.

"I wasn't allowed any money for myself. He would spend £200 a week at a strip club; I had to give a comprehensive budget of everything I was spending"

She added that the worst cases of domestic abuse, where there was intimidation "over a long period of time", would carry a jail term, although no maximum sentences had yet been drawn up.

Less serious examples are likely to be dealt with by community orders or fines.

The number of domestic abuse cases referred by police for prosecution reached a record high of 103,500 last year.

Conviction rates for this type of crime have increased from just under 60 per cent in 2005–06 to nearly 75 per cent in 2013–14, according to the Home Office. Polly Neate, the chief executive of Women's Aid, said: "This is a vital step forward for victims of domestic violence.

"Two women a week are killed by domestic violence, and in our experience of working with survivors, coercive controlling behaviour is at the heart of the most dangerous abuse."

Prof. David Wilson, a criminologist at Birmingham City University, supported the move, but warned that the new offence could pose initial legal problems.

"The dividing line between abuse and criminality is often one that is difficult to measure," he said.

Peter Lodder QC, a criminal barrister, added: "The law can be a blunt instrument and if you are talking about how people conduct their private lives the criminal law is not always the best way to control that.

"Extreme cases may be obvious but the difficulty may come with where one draws the line."

⇨ For advice on combating domestic abuse contact the National Domestic Violence Helpline on 0808 2000 247. If you are a perpetrator of domestic violence and wish to seek help call Respect on 0808 802 4040. For advice on abuse within lesbian and gay relationships contact Broken Rainbow on 0300 999 5428.

20 August 2014

⇨ The above information is reprinted with kind permission from *The Telegraph*. Please visit www. telegraph.co.uk for further information.

Don't compare male circumcision with FGM

The common practice of cutting a boy's foreskin for religious reasons bears no relation to the abominable act of FGM, writes Simon Hochhauser.

By Simon Hochhauser, Co-Chairman of Milah UK

Last week, the Girl Summit conference in London rightly focused the news agenda's attention on female genital mutilation (FGM). Hosted by David Cameron and led by Theresa May and Justine Greening, the conference was the first of its kind in the UK – a country where an estimated 66,000 women are living with the consequences of a barbarically intrusive practice.

FGM, which involves the partial or complete removal of the genitalia, is a crime because it is abhorrent by any measure. It subjugates women, makes intercourse extremely difficult and painful, and can be the cause of a number of serious medical complications, including not only haemorrhage but also urinary retention, urinary infection, wound infection and septicaemia. Sadly, in the countries where it is most widely performed, hygiene is poor, and thus both hepatitis and tetanus have also resulted.

Contrary to what Neil Lyndon wrote yesterday in *Telegraph Men*, none of this is comparable to the practice of male religious circumcision. Mr Lyndon would have us believe that the practice – known as 'Brit Milah' in the Jewish community – should be considered in the same light as FGM. It's a bizarre argument to make, rather like comparing ear piercing with sawing off a person's entire ear with a rusty hacksaw.

Brit Milah is a minor procedure. When carried out by a trained practitioner in a clean environment it has no recognised negative impact on the child or on the rest of his life. Of course there are risks associated with any such procedure. Mr Lyndon points to deaths of Angelo Ofori-Mintah and Goodluck Caubergs, who both bled to death after undergoing circumcision. But it is disingenuous to suggest that these two isolated tragedies, which (incidentally) bear no resemblance to conventional Brit Milah as it is carried out today, are indicative of a widespread problem.

The facts speak for themselves. According to the World Health Organization, circumcision of male babies results in "a very low rate of adverse events, which are usually minor (0.2–0.4%)". These figures would no doubt be much lower still if they referred only to properly regulated and responsibly carried out circumcisions.

Mr Lyndon's suggestion is that, while a third of the male population of the planet is circumcised, the practice is not challenged in the same way as FGM has been because culturally we are not 'comfortable' taking issue with it. I would like to offer a slightly different explanation: we're very happy! There are no international movements calling for an end to circumcision because the billions of men around the planet who have been circumcised have not experienced any negative effects. In fact, the religious and cultural significance of the practice means that, to them, it is an overwhelmingly positive event. Put simply, circumcision has not had an adverse impact on their lives.

Maybe there are some people who do consider it to have been a negative experience and who feel that they would have liked to have had the choice. But I would contend that there would be many, many more people who would feel much more aggrieved if they had been prevented from undergoing the procedure as an infant, as mandated by their faith.

Nevertheless, both groups of people have rights which must be respected, so how should we reconcile them?

Normal practice, where there is a question about the religious and/or physical well-being of an infant, is to defer to their parents, who we tend to assume have the best interests of their child at heart. Parents don't always get it right – hence the campaigns against FGM – but any equivalent campaign against male circumcision would have to be accompanied by an overwhelming body of objective scientific evidence that demonstrated significant harm to the child. As far as circumcision goes, there is no such evidence. Some scientists even claim that it is medically beneficial.

Mr Lyndon dismissively characterises the view that male religious circumcision isn't comparable to FGM as "nitwit feminism in which males are of no consequence at all". I disagree entirely. Given the blindingly obvious practical and medical differences between the procedures, it is deeply irresponsible to attribute the different treatment of these topics as some sort of underhanded feminist conspiracy. To do so threatens simultaneously to generate unwarranted attacks on religious practice, and undermine the important campaign against FGM.

30 July 2014

Elder abuse

Many older people experience some form of abuse in the home.

Elder abuse is a single or repeated act, or lack of appropriate action, occurring within any relationship where there is an expectation of trust that causes harm or distress to an older person. Elder abuse includes physical, sexual, psychological, emotional, financial and material abuse; abandonment; neglect and serious loss of dignity and respect.

Key facts

National surveys conducted in predominantly high-income countries find wide variation in rates of abuse in the preceding 12 months among adults aged over 60 years, ranging from 0.8% in Spain and 2.6% in the United Kingdom to upwards of 18% in Israel, 23.8% in Austria and 32% in Belgium.

Elder abuse can lead to serious physical injuries and long-term psychological consequences, including depression and anxiety.

Elder abuse is predicted to increase as many countries are experiencing rapidly ageing populations.

Findings from the survey

Although public and professional information campaigns to raise awareness about elder abuse are reported in many countries, elder abuse is one of the least-investigated types of violence in national surveys, and one of the least addressed in national action plans.

Prevention approaches

Strategies to prevent elder abuse include efforts to raise professional awareness and train practitioners; inform the public about how to identify the signs and symptoms of elder abuse and where help can be obtained, and

improving policies and practices in residential care facilities for elderly people. There is, however, very little research on the effectiveness of any such programmes in preventing elder abuse, and this is a critical gap to fill.

⇨ The above information is an extract from the *Global status report on violence prevention 2014* (GSRVP 2014), pages 78–79 (http://www.who.int/violence_ injury_prevention/violence/status_report/2014/ report/report/en/).

© World Health Organization 2016

Proportion of countries that reported implementing a particular strategy

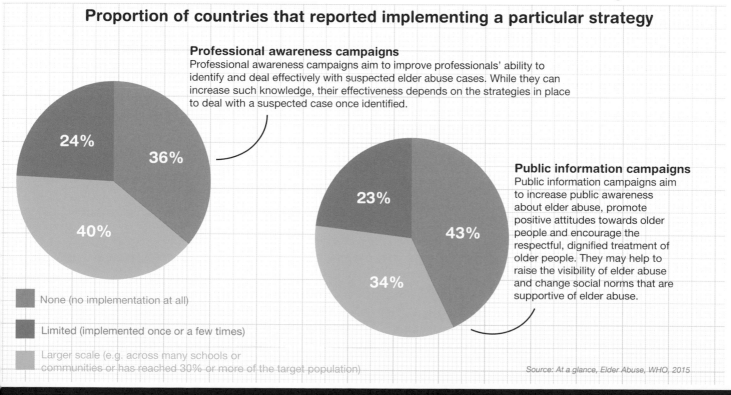

Professional awareness campaigns
Professional awareness campaigns aim to improve professionals' ability to identify and deal effectively with suspected elder abuse cases. While they can increase such knowledge, their effectiveness depends on the strategies in place to deal with a suspected case once identified.

24%
36%
40%

23%
43%
34%

Public information campaigns
Public information campaigns aim to increase public awareness about elder abuse, promote positive attitudes towards older people and encourage the respectful, dignified treatment of older people. They may help to raise the visibility of elder abuse and change social norms that are supportive of elder abuse.

None (no implementation at all)

Limited (implemented once or a few times)

Larger scale (e.g. across many schools or communities or has reached 30% or more of the target population)

Source: At a glance, Elder Abuse, WHO, 2015

Male victims of women's violence fear not being believed

Men who receive help from crisis centres are mostly satisfied with the help they get. But they fear that nobody will believe that they've been abused by a woman.

By Eivor Maeland

"There is little difference between how men and women handle being exposed to domestic violence," says criminologist Yngvil Grøvdal.

She is one of the researchers behind the report *Men at crisis centres* (*Menn på krisesenter*), based on qualitative interviews with 16 men. 14 of them were exposed to violence from a female partner, while two were exposed to violence from male partners.

The 16 men were recruited to the survey through the three crisis centres with most male users at the time of the survey in 2012.

In the new report, Grøvdal and her colleague Wenche Jonassen from Norwegian Centre for Violence and Traumatic Stress Studies (NKVTS) look at men who are victims of domestic violence and their experiences with crisis centres.

"As far as we know, Norway is the only country where men are legally entitled to access at crisis centres," says Grøvdal.

The men

Ten of the interviewees in the report were ethnic Norwegians, one was a European and five were originally from non-western countries. Half of the men who were victims of female violence had children with the woman. All except two had ended their relationship with the abuser when they were interviewed.

The men were generally satisfied with their experiences with the staff at the crisis centres. In particular, they were impressed by the way the staff made the most out of limited or lacking resources.

"All in all, the men were very satisfied with the staff at the crisis centres and their efforts," says Grøvdal.

"This may be partly due to the selection. The crisis centres would probably not have recruited people they know are unhappy with the work they do. But it also appears that these men had low expectations in the first place. This may be due to their perception of crisis centres, but some of them had bad experiences from the general support system. This may lead to lower expectations the next time you seek help," she says.

The universally human

Six years ago, in January 2010, the Crisis Centre Act was passed. From then on, the municipalities have been responsible for the crisis centres and access has become gender neutral.

"Men who are exposed to domestic violence have many of the same needs as female victims of domestic violence. Something universally human seems to come into play when you are exposed to violence from your partner or someone you have chosen to share your life with. This is probably one of the reasons why the competence at the crisis centres is perceived as relevant for men as well as for women," says Grøvdal.

Fear of more violence, shame, anxiety related to how the children will handle the situation, and warm feelings for the violent abuser are reoccurring elements in both men's and women's stories about their lives with violence.

Shameful

Several of the men in the survey expressed shame of being victims of violence from a woman. It doesn't agree with their own or society's ideas of what men are or are supposed to be.

"In my culture it is shameful to tell someone that I've been hit by a woman. No one would believe it either. Neither did I dare to return the violence, in fear of being deported [out of the country]."

This is a quote from "David", an African man in his thirties. David's wife came to Norway before him, and worked in a nursing home. When David came to Norway on family reunification, he had problems getting work and getting integrated into Norwegian society. His wife eventually started taking control of his life, she often yelled at him, and threatened him by saying that her father and brothers would beat him up. She also became violent herself: during a fight she spat him in the face, hit him in the face with a flat hand and she threatened him with a knife several times.

With the proviso that such categories are problematic, the researchers have categorised the violence into aggravated violence, less aggravated violence and mental abuse. One example of aggravated violence from the research material was one who had his eye torn out. Other examples of aggravated violence may be when the abuser uses a knife and reoccurring violent episodes. So-called less aggravated violence is violence that causes low risk of physical damage such as pulling the hair, spitting, pinching and so on.

"Although many of the reactions and actions from the interviewed men are similar to those of women in the same situation, men appear to be more worried about not being believed when they talk about the violence than women are," says Grøvdal.

"Several said that no one would believe that they had been victims of violence from a woman. Some said their partner had told them that no one would believe them."

The ridiculed victim

The men's fear of not being believed is not unfounded.

"Due to this survey we now know that the crisis centres have encountered police who don't take men seriously and that the men themselves experience not being taken seriously by The Norwegian Welfare and Labour Administration (NAV) and the Child Welfare Service," says Grøvdal.

She also refers to other research which shows that men face problems being taken seriously when they say that they have been abused by a female partner.

Among of the research Grøvdal is referring to is the book *The invisible violence: men who are victims of domestic violence by women* (*Den usynliggjorte volden: om menn som utsettes for partnervold fra kvinner*) from 2013, in which Tove Ingebjørg Fjell, professor of Cultural History at the University of Bergen, has interviewed several male victims of domestic violence.

Fjell has also written an article about how men who are victims of violence from a female partner are often ridiculed in comedy shows.

"But we don't find it as amusing if a man does the same to a woman," says Grøvdal.

Women can also take up arms

On average, men are physically stronger than women, thus many people believe that women's violence cannot be very serious. What do you think about these attitudes?

"In a way this makes women less all-human, if we claim that they're incapable of performing actions that we consider unacceptable. Women can also take up arms or weapon-like objects. The action can happen very sudden, not giving the man the opportunity to defend himself. Moreover, some men are afraid to defend themselves as they fear that this will be used against them," says Grøvdal.

"We also know that violence can come like a bolt from the blue."

One of the men in the study experienced his partner using a knife against him, another woman burned her partner with a hot object, possibly an iron – he couldn't see it, as she attacked him from behind.

"Neither is it true that all women are weaker than all men," Grøvdal points out.

"We know that some men, although not as many as women, are exposed to life-threatening violence. And we need to deal with that."

Gender segregated crisis centres

The Norwegian Institute for Welfare and Ageing's (NOVA) evaluation of crisis centres shows that women are offered different services than men are. The women are to a much higher degree part of a community.

"Many men at the crisis centres live alone. The children who accompany their father to the crisis centre are not offered the same services as children accompanying their mother. The services offered to the women often include professional services for the children, whereas the children accompanying the men risk being more isolated," says Grøvdal.

In the consultation papers to the Crisis Centre Act, an important requirement was that men and women were to live completely separated at the crisis centres. In many places, this means that the men are geographically separated from the women, often placed in apartments or, in some cases, hotel rooms which are rented for a shorter period of time.

"I think it is both interesting and paradoxical that the crisis centres are concerned that the women who have been victims of violence from a male partner should not have to meet any men at all, whereas nobody seems to care if men who have been victims of violence from a female partner have to meet women. This probably has to do with gender stereotypes," says Grøvdal.

Some of the staff also experienced that as a result of the 2010 Act they were assigned more tasks without

being provided increased funding accordingly.

The crisis centre's competence

The crisis centres were established in the 1970s by women who had been exposed to domestic violence and wanted to help other women in similar situations. They wanted domestic violence and the abuse of women to be regarded as a public, not a private, problem.

Today we talk about violence within close relations and domestic violence in order to emphasise that 'he' is not always the abuser and 'she' is not always the victim.

"We know from research that more women than men are exposed to aggravated violence and that more women than men are killed by their partner. But this doesn't mean that men cannot be victims of this type of violence," says Grøvdal.

She calls for more research on how the police and staff within the health and social services understand gender in general and on how they treat men who have been exposed to domestic violence in particular.

"It is problematic if we pit men who have been exposed to domestic violence against women in similar situations. Everyone who needs it should receive protection and help regardless of whether they're men or women."

Translated by Cathinka Dahl Hambro

28 October 2015

Reference:

Yngvil Grøvdal and Wenche Jonassen: *Menn på krisesenter* (*Men at Crisis Centres*). Report 5/2015. Norwegian Centre for Violence and Traumatic Stress Studies (NKVTS).

The issue of violence in teenage relationships

Violence in adolescent relationships is a growing concern for many. Expert Mark Bowles examines the evidence, prevalence and impact of this kind of violence on young people – and looks at what schools can do to play their part in tackling the problem.

Violence in romantic relationships has been long thought to be an adult issue. However, significant evidence from the US exists in relation to its prevalence within adolescent relationships and an understanding of its impact is building in the UK.

Because domestic violence is often perceived as an adult issue, the focus of most research has been on adults and the impact of domestic abuse on their wider families[1][2]. More recently, intimate partner violence among young people has been highlighted as "an understudied area of maltreatment in the UK" and this omission has significantly hampered the development of theoretical understanding and effective prevention programmes[3].

Given the understanding of adolescence as a critical developmental period and the substantial amount of research in relation to adolescence, it is surprising that so little is known about this social problem of violence in adolescent intimate relationships.

Young people involved in dating violence are at higher risk of further violence in future relationships, riskier sexual behaviour[4] and increased rates of substance use and eating disorders[5].

Prevalence

Although a substantive body of UK evidence exists on adult women's, and to a lesser extent children's, experiences of domestic violence[1][2], we know little about teenagers' own experiences of partner violence. Most of the empirical evidence on teenage partner violence is derived from US studies.

These findings suggest that boys and girls use similar levels of physical and emotional violence towards their partners[6], resulting in propositions that teenage partner violence demonstrates a greater degree of gender symmetry compared to adult domestic violence where women are predominantly the victim.

However, research also shows that girls are more likely to be the recipient of serious physical and sexual violence than boys. In addition, while both boys and girls use verbal violence and control mechanisms, the impact of these on girls appears to be much greater than on boys[7].

Rates of relationship abuse vary according to age, sex and previous experience of violence[8]. The prevalence of relationship violence is higher in adolescents than in adults, with females aged 12 to 18 years having the highest victimisation rate[9].

Approximately 20 per cent of young women have experienced violence from a dating partner[10] and first episodes of violence frequently occur in adolescence[11].

The NSPCC has tried to bridge this gap in the UK evidence-base in part through its 2009 paper *Partner exploitation and violence in teenage intimate relationships*[12].

This multi-method study collected survey responses from 1,353 young people aged between 13 and 17 and conducted qualitative interviews with 62 girls and 29 boys. It found that 18 per cent of boys and 25 per cent of girls reported some form of physical partner violence.

While limited in its size, this study does indicate that adolescent dating violence is a potentially significant child welfare problem in the UK.

Terminology

Most of the US and wider international literature has adopted the term 'dating' to describe this area of work. However, this terminology does not transfer well to the UK context, as young people do not use or recognise this term.

In addition, 'dating' seems to imply a degree of formality which does not necessarily reflect the diverse range of young people's intimate encounters and relationships. Experts have argued that research needs to reflect the fluidity of teenage relationships, producing typologies to describe different teenage intimate encounters[13].

Researchers also warn that teenagers use specific terms such as 'hanging out', 'hooked up', 'being sprung' and 'being friends with privileges', and that such terms undoubtedly vary by county, region, gender, age and ethnicity[3].

Also, there are clear problems when

1 *Children's Perspectives on Domestic Violence*, Mullender et al (2002).

2 *Domestic Violence: Making it through the criminal justice system*, University of Sunderland and the Northern Rock Foundation; Hester, M (2006).

3 *Dating Violence Among Adolescents Article: Prevalence, Gender Distribution, and Prevention Program Effectiveness*, Hickman et al (2004).

4 *Dating Violence Among Urban, Minority, Middle School Youth and Associated Sexual Risk Behaviors and Substance Use*, Lormand, Donna et al, Journal of School Health 83.6 (2013).

5 *Dating Violence Against Adolescent Girls and Associated Substance Use, Unhealthy Weight Control, Sexual Risk Behavior, Pregnancy, and Suicidality*, Silverman JG, Raj A, Mucci LA, Hathaway JE, Journal of the American Medical Association (2001).

6 *Adolescent Dating Violence: Do adolescents follow in their friends', or their parents', footsteps?*, Foshee et al (2004).

7 *"If It Hurts You, Then It Is Not a Joke": Adolescents' ideas about girls' and boys' use and experience of abusive behavior in dating relationships*, Sears et al (2006).

8 *An Evaluation of Safe Dates, an Adolescent Dating Violence Prevention Program*, Foshee et al (1998).

9 *Domestic Violence: Findings from a new British Crime Survey self-completion questionnaire*, Home Office (1999).

10 *Teen Dating Violence*, O'Keefe, Brockopp, Chew (1986).

11 *Romance and Violence in Dating Relationships*, Henton et al (1983).

12 *Partner Exploitation and Violence in Teenage Intimate Relationships*, NSPCC (2009): http://bit.ly/1RBOZgp

13 *Dating Experiences of Bullies in Early Adolescence*, Connolly et al, Child Maltreatment (2000); Making Meaning of Relationships: Young women's experiences and understandings of dating violence. Chung, D (2007).

describing domestic abuse among young people, since there are myriad terms attached to this behaviour and they are mostly focused on abuse in adult relationships. Much of the evidence, mainly from the US, focuses on using 'dating violence', which does not take into account other forms of abuse young people experience. Other terms include 'intimate partner violence or abuse' and 'teenage partner violence or abuse'.

Impact among young people

What we know about teenage partner violence testifies to its serious consequences for the well-being of victims and their future life prospects. Relationship abuse negatively impacts on young people's well-being, initiating feelings of anger, hurt and fear[14].

More girls than boys report severe emotional reaction, fear and physical injuries; more boys report being unperturbed[15]. One study found that more than half of victims reported feeling 'bad about themselves' alongside feelings of anger, sadness, depression and low self-esteem[16].

For some, partner abuse is a continuation of violence in their lives, and, for others, it is their first experience of this type of behaviour. Some studies have indicated that abuse in adolescent relationships can be a precursor for abuse in adult relationships[17].

Risk factors

The research has identified some risk factors, which include previous experiences of parental domestic violence, physical and sexual abuse, and violent peer groups[10 14 18].

While less researched, it appears that parental neglect, especially lack of supervision and involvement/interest in their teenage children's lives, also

has a negative impact on young people's vulnerability to partner violence[19], although what constitutes 'neglect' for adolescents has still to be fully explored within the research literature.

However, the research has identified key protective factors, which include:

⇨ Achievement at school.

⇨ Having a safe haven.

⇨ Support from positive role-models – in school and outside of school.

⇨ Assertiveness (both internal and external).

⇨ Sense of physical, emotional and economic security.

What can schools and teachers do?

As outlined above, this is a growing area of study, especially in the UK. Work has been undertaken however, not least by the NSPCC[13] that does suggest young people in the UK suffer from violence in adolescent relationships at a comparable level to their US peers.

The expansion of intervention programmes related to the teaching of consent specifically, and healthy relationships more generally, should be welcomed.

However, the majority of these programmes will operate only at the universal level, delivering interventions across entire youth population groups. As with all universal programmes, it is hard to see how universal messages will be effective for young people already in abusive peer relationships.

It would seem however that a need for higher-level intervention programmes for young people who are experiencing abuse and violence in their own romantic relationships should be considered. To ensure their effectiveness, the provision of screening and assessment tools to help professionals identify these young people should also be considered as part of any targeted intervention programmes.

Schools have a vital role, not only to educate their young people in relation to this issue, but to identify

those experiencing this issue or at an increased risk. Schools and teachers could ensure that:

⇨ Training on domestic abuse is provided to all staff with a specific focus on young people.

⇨ Training includes risk and protective factors related to adolescent dating violence.

⇨ Consideration is given to the specific needs of children experiencing domestic abuse.

⇨ Family interventions are supported by and where appropriate delivered within the school.

⇨ Timely and appropriate referrals to social care and/or specialist services are made for young people and families.

⇨ Universal and targeted programmes and interventions are implemented, ensuring that the most appropriate support can be offered.

⇨ The teaching of healthy relationships and consent is an embedded part of the schools PSHE provision (universal provision).

⇨ The implementation of an evidence-based and fully evaluated life-skills programme focused on vulnerable young people is considered (targeted provision).

⇨ When using outside agencies and speakers care is taken to ensure that delivery is consummate with the available evidence-base.

Mark Bowles is director of The Training Effect, a provider of health-based interventions on topics such as substance misuse, families with complex needs, risk-taking behaviour, emotional and mental health.

2 July 2015

⇨ The above information is reprinted with kind permission from The Training Effect. Please visit www.thetrainingeffect.co.uk for further information.

14   *Victims of Dating Violence Among High School Students: Are the predictors different for males and females?* O'Keefe M and Treister L, Violence Against Women (1998)

15 *Dating Abuse: Prevalence, consequences, and predictors,* Foshee et al (1996).

16 *Risk Factors Associated with Date Rape and Sexual Assault of Adolescent Girls,* Vicary et al, Journal of Adolescence (1995).

17 *Can We Prevent the Hitting? Recommendations for preventing intimate partner violence between young adults,* O'Leary et al (1989).

18 *Importance of Gender and Attitudes about Violence in the Relationship between Exposure to Interparental Violence and the Perpetration of Teen Dating Violence,* Wolfe et al, Child Abuse and Neglect (2013)

19 *Parenting Processes and Dating Violence: The mediating role of self- esteem in low and high SES adolescents,* Pflieger and Vazsony, Journal of Adolescence (2006).

Abuse in teenage relationships

If you're in a relationship and you feel unhappy about or frightened by the way your partner treats you, you don't have to put up with it.

It can be hard to know what's 'normal' in a relationship. It can take time to get to know each other and discover what works for you both.

But there's one thing that's for sure: abusive or violent behaviour is not acceptable. If it's happening to you, it's OK to ask for help and advice.

Partner abuse can happen to anyone of any age, culture or religion. It can happen to boys or girls, but it's much more likely to happen to girls. Young people in same-sex relationships are also more likely to be affected.

Tink Palmer, a social worker who works with people who have been abused, says: "No-one should have to put up with violence in any form. If it's happening to you, talk to a person you trust, such as a parent, a trusted adult or a friend. Don't hold it in – talk to someone."

What is abuse in a relationship?

Abuse can involve physical violence, such as hitting, kicking, pushing, slapping or pressuring you into sex.

But there are other forms of abuse, too.

Emotional and verbal abuse can involve your boyfriend or girlfriend:

⇨ saying things that make you feel small, whether you're alone or in front of other people

⇨ pressuring you to do things you don't want to do, including sexual things

⇨ checking up on you all the time to find out where you are and who you're with – for example, texting or calling you a lot if you're out with your friends

⇨ threatening to hurt you or someone close to you, including pets.

As well as happening when you're together, emotional and verbal abuse can happen on the phone or on the Internet.

Behaviour like this is not about love. It's about someone controlling you and making you behave how they want. People who abuse a partner verbally or emotionally may turn to violence later on in the relationship. This kind of controlling behaviour is a big warning sign.

Behaviour like this is not OK, even if some people tell you it is. Violence and abuse in relationships is not normal, it is not 'just the way things are' or 'messing around'. It's a serious issue.

Being hurt emotionally and physically can harm your self-esteem and make you feel anxious, depressed or ill. Young people who are abused can also develop eating disorders, problems with alcohol and drugs, and be at risk of sexually transmitted infections and pregnancy from sexual abuse.

Getting help for abuse

If you're in a controlling or abusive relationship and you want help, don't be scared to talk to someone about it. Remember, it's not your fault, no matter what anyone says, and it is far better to talk about it with someone. It doesn't matter if you've been drinking or what you've been wearing. There is no excuse.

It can be difficult to find the right words to ask for help. Try asking someone whether you can talk to them about something. Tell them you need some help or that something is happening and you don't know what to do.

There are several people you might talk to, such as:

⇨ an adult mentor or a favourite teacher at school

⇨ your mum, dad or another trusted adult – perhaps a friend's mum

⇨ an adviser on a helpline such as ChildLine (0800 1111)

⇨ a GP or nurse

⇨ a friend.

And remember, try again if you don't get the response you think you need. If you are in immediate danger, call 999.

If you think a friend is being abused

If you think a friend might be experiencing abuse, talk to them. "Keep calm, and don't be judgmental or condemning," says Palmer. "It can be difficult to talk to a friend, but try. If you're concerned, don't worry that you might be wrong, worry that you might be right."

Try asking your friend if you can talk about something. Tell them you're worried about them and ask them whether everything is OK. Listen to them and let them know that nobody has to put up with abuse.

If they have been hurt, offer to go to the doctor with them. Have the number of a useful helpline, such as ChildLine on 0800 1111, ready to give to them.

Your friend might be angry or upset with you for a while, but they will know you care and you might have helped them realise they can get help.

If you're abusing someone

If you're abusing your partner or you're worried that you might, you can call ChildLine on 0800 1111 or talk to a trusted adult.

"Recognising that your behaviour is wrong is the first step to stopping it. But you may need help to stop," says Palmer.

Sometimes the things that cause abusive behaviour, such as feelings about things that happened in the past, can be very powerful. "We can't always stop things on our own, or straight away," says Palmer. "We do need help, which is why it's important to talk to someone."

16 July 2014

⇨ The above information is reprinted with kind permission from NHS Choices. Please visit www.nhs.uk for further information.

© Crown copyright 2016

Pets caught up in domestic violence

It is becoming more and more common that family pets are used as a tool to manipulate and control victims of domestic violence. In addition, increasing research and clinical evidence suggests that there are inter-relationships, commonly referred to as 'links', between the abuse of children, vulnerable adults and animals. A better understanding of these links can help to protect victims, both human and animal, and promote their welfare.

The Links Group aims to raise awareness of the 'links' to all professionals in the hope that agencies will work together to help prevent related cases from going undetected.

Abuse to children, vulnerable adults or animals can have damaging and devastating effects for the victims, their families and wider society. If you are faced with this situation and don't know where to turn, you should know that there are organisations that can give you and your family safe refuge, whilst at the same time looking after the family pet.

It has been shown that:

⇨ Where serious animal abuse has occurred in a household there may be an increased likelihood that some other form of family violence is also occurring.

⇨ It is also apparent that children may be at increased risk of abuse in this environment.

⇨ Acts of animal abuse may in some circumstances be used to coerce, control and intimidate a partner and children to remain in, or be silent about, their abusive situation. The threat or actual abuse of a pet can prevent victims from leaving situations of domestic violence.

An actual quote:

"He held my daughters' pets out of the upstairs window, and threatened to drop them if we did not return home."

In a survey by pet fostering charity Paws for Kids:

⇨ 66% said their abuser had threatened to harm their pets

⇨ 94% said if there had been a pet fostering service it would have made it easier for them to leave the violence, and so spare themselves and their children more abuse.

How it works

Petlink Raystede Home for Animal Welfare in East Sussex and part of The Links Group describe their procedure, "We take referrals from both agencies and/or directly from the owner, providing they can provide confirmation that they are fleeing domestic violence, i.e. an email or letter from a case worker, the police or social services. We will then ask you to complete a variety of forms which include pet information form and a legal contract. Once this information has been received we will endeavour to place your pet temporarily in a loving family home with a volunteer foster carer. Your pet will be reunited with you once you are settled and are able to have it back."

An actual story:

Joanna's domestic violence key worker contacted the Pet Fostering Service explaining she had been working with Joanna for the past six months, but Joanna would not leave her violent home until something could be sorted out for her two beloved dogs, Ruby and Toby. Referral forms were faxed and returned the same day. Arrangements were made to meet Joanna with Ruby and Toby the following day while she was on her way to the refuge. Obviously, she was very upset about parting with them, but knew it was the only way they would all be safe. Ruby and Toby jumped into the van and settled down together.

On arrival at the foster carer's house Ruby and Toby explored their new environment and within a couple of hours had made themselves quite at home, with Ruby on the sofa and Toby curled up on the rug in front of the fire. Joanna was offered a property within a few months and once she had settled in, was reunited her with her dogs.

⇨ The above information is reprinted with kind permission from the Pet Owners Association. Please visit www.pet-owners.co.uk for further information.

© Pet Owners Association 2016

"Domestic abuse is everyone's problem": why criminalising coercive control just isn't enough

Following their consultation "strengthening the Law on Domestic Abuse", the Government plans to introduce a law on domestic abuse which criminalises 'coercive control'.

By Siobhan Weare

The legislation will make controlling and coercive behaviour between those in an intimate relationship a criminal offence. Introducing such legislation is not sufficient to combat the issue of domestic abuse unless it is supported by an improvement in the responses of criminal justice agencies to abuse, and increased investment in support services for victims.

Currently, domestic abuse is not criminalised as a specific offence; however, victims of physical violence are offered protection under existing criminal offences. Protection is also offered under civil law in the form of non-molestation and occupation orders. The police have been given additional powers through the Domestic Violence Disclosure Scheme (Clare's Law), to disclose information on request about whether an individual's partner has a history of perpetrating domestic violence. The police can also issue Domestic Violence Protection Notices, placing restrictions on the perpetrator contacting the victim and providing immediate emergency protection to victims.

Creating an offence of coercive control will bring the law in line with the government's existing non-statutory definition of domestic abuse. In creating this offence the Government hopes that it will 'help victims identify the behaviour they are suffering as wrong and encourage them to report it, and cause perpetrators to rethink their controlling behaviour'. The Government acknowledges that currently the police response to non-violent domestic abuse is largely inadequate, and by explicitly acknowledging coercive and controlling behaviour as an offence anticipates that this form of abuse will be taken more seriously.

Any steps taken to address the issue of domestic abuse are commendable, but simply criminalising coercive control is not a sufficient response. As discussed above, there are already numerous laws used to protect victims of domestic abuse. However, evidence suggests that these existing legal provisions are not being used effectively enough, and therefore, if a new offence of coercive control is introduced, will it suffer the same ineffective fate of its predecessors?

The Government hopes that by creating an offence of coercive control, reporting rates of domestic abuse will increase. Statistics from the United States, where similar laws have been introduced in some states, indicate a 50% increase in reporting rates. In order for victims to feel able to report their abuse, they need confidence in the responses of criminal justice agencies. A recent report by Her Majesty's Inspectorate of Constabularies (HMIC) highlighted a number of significant failings in police responses to victims of domestic abuse. The report indicated that victims who reported their abuse to the police sometimes felt they were not believed, that specialist domestic violence units in police forces are often under-resourced and overwhelmed, and that there are unacceptable variations when charging perpetrators with offences (https://www.justiceinspectorates.gov.uk/hmic/wp-content/uploads/2014/04/improving-the-police-response-to-domestic-abuse.pdf). It is clear that urgent improvements are needed in the police response to domestic abuse to secure more prosecutions under existing legislation and to increase confidence in the criminal justice process.

Within the justice system there needs to be an eradication of the damaging stereotypes which continue to surround victims of domestic abuse. Victims are stereotyped as being female, abused in the context of a heterosexual relationship, with the abuser being their male partner or ex-partner. Although this is the context within which the majority of domestic abuse takes place, a significant minority of cases involve male victims abused by their female partner, or domestic abuse taking place in same-sex relationships. Domestic abuse within these contexts is often overlooked, thus discouraging these victims from coming forward for fear that they will not be believed. Indeed, research conducted by the charity ManKind has highlighted that "male victims (29%) are nearly twice as likely than women (17%) to not tell anyone about the partner abuse". There is also a continuing issue within the justice system of stereotypes of abuse victims more generally. Victims of domestic abuse who fail to conform to particular stereotypes that dictate that they should be meek and passive in the face of the abuse have their status as victims regularly called into question.

Alongside creating an offence of coercive control, more investment also needs to be made in the services that provide support to victims of domestic abuse. Currently only victims who are at the highest risk of serious harm from their partners or ex-partners can access support from Independent Domestic Violence Advisors (IDVAs). Their invaluable support can include creating safety plans for the victim to leave their abusive partner and supporting the victim in giving evidence in court. The

number of IDVAs has decreased as a result of funding cuts and they are not available to those who are assessed as being at low to medium risk of serious harm. Domestic violence charities and organisations, who are often funded by local government, have seen significant reductions in funding. Since 2010, one in six specialist refuges has been lost due to funding cuts and 48% of the 167 domestic violence services in England are running their services without government funding. In response to a campaign by Women's Aid, the Government has committed £10 million to prevent the closure of specialist refuges. However, there are still concerns that this is insufficient to offer the degree of support needed for victims.

With 1.1 million women and 720,000 men reporting domestic violence in the past year, domestic abuse is a significant societal issue. Simply

creating new legislation will not combat this problem. Alongside creating an offence of coercive control, more work needs to be done in improving justice agencies' responses to domestic abuse, supported by investment in the support services so valuable to victims of abuse. As one victim of domestic abuse stated on BBC *Panorama*'s *Domestic Abuse: Caught on Camera*; "domestic abuse is everyone's problem" – it's about time that this was truly reflected in the governmental and justice system's responses to this form of abuse.

17 December 2014

⇨ The above information is reprinted with kind permission from Lancaster University. Please visit www.lancaster.ac.uk for further information.

New law to tackle revenge porn

People who maliciously share sexually explicit pictures of former partners will face prosecution under new laws.

Revenge porn – the distribution of a private sexual image of someone without their consent and with the intention of causing them distress – will be made a specific offence in the Criminal Justice and Courts Bill, which is currently going through Parliament.

Justice Secretary Chris Grayling said:

"The fact that there are individuals who are cruelly distributing intimate pictures of their former partners without their consent is almost beyond belief.

"We want those who fall victim to this type of disgusting behaviour to know that we are on their side and will do everything we can to bring offenders to justice.

"That is why we will change the law and make it absolutely clear to those who act in this way that they could face prison."

Minister for Women and Equalities Nicky Morgan said:

"Circulating intimate photos of an individual without their consent is never acceptable. People are entitled to expect a reasonable level of respect and privacy.

"It is right that those who do circulate these images are held to account, and that we educate young people to the hurt that can be caused by breaking this trust."

The change will cover the sharing of images both online and offline. It will mean that images posted to social networking sites such as Facebook and Twitter will be caught by the offence, as well as those that are shared via text message. Images shared via e-mail, on a website or the distribution of physical copies will also be caught. Those convicted will face a maximum sentence of two years in prison.

The offence will cover photographs or films which show people engaged in sexual activity or depicted in a sexual way or with their genitals

exposed, where what is shown would not usually be seen in public. Victims and others will be able to report offences to the police to investigate. Officers will work with the Crown Prosecution Service to take forward cases for prosecution.

Those found to have committed a sexual offence can continue

to be prosecuted under existing legislation, which can lead to sentences of up to 14 years in prison.

The change in the law will be made via an amendment to the Criminal Justice and Courts Bill, which includes a number of measures to toughen up sentencing.

These include ending automatic half-way point release for criminals convicted of rape or attempted rape of a child, or serious terrorism offences, and ensuring that all offenders who receive the tough Extended Determinate Sentence (EDS) are no longer automatically released two-thirds of the way through their custodial term.

Notes to editors

Sending images of this kind may, depending on the circumstances, be an offence under the Communications Act 2003 or the Malicious Communications Act 1988. Behaviour of this kind, if repeated, may also amount to an offence of harassment under the Protection from Harassment Act 1997.

Specific legislation also applies to the making, dissemination or possession of indecent photographs of children under the age of 18.

The maximum penalty for possession of indecent photographs of children is five years in prison.

Creation and distribution of such photographs carries a maximum penalty of ten years.

If anyone has been a victim of this kind of behaviour they should get in touch with the police immediately.

Follow the Ministry of Justice on Twitter @MoJPress and get involved in the discussion using #revengeporn.

For more information contact the Ministry of Justice Press Office on 0203 334 3536.

12 October 2014

⇨ The above information is reprinted with kind permission from the Ministry of Justice and The Rt Hon. Chris Grayling MP. Please visit www.gov.uk for further information.

Getting it right first time

Executive summary from the report by SafeLives.

From a response to high-risk victims to a response for all victims and children

The SafeLives approach has transformed how high-risk domestic abuse is addressed in the UK. Last year our work supported more than 50,000 adults parenting around 70,000 children, all of whom were living with high-risk abuse. More than 60% of victims receiving support through this approach reported that the abuse stopped.

But, of course, this system is effective only for victims of high-risk domestic abuse. It is not – nor was it intended to be – a response to all victims and their families. The clarity of the national approach to high-risk victims has not been matched by a similar focus on other victims and family members. And few areas take a strategic overview of how they respond to domestic abuse.

SafeLives is starting a programme to understand how to create the full system change we need to stop domestic abuse and save lives. We will start by looking at how we can identify every family where there is domestic abuse as quickly as possible – the topic of this article.

We have to find every family where there is domestic abuse much more quickly

Why do we need to find families earlier?

The impact of domestic abuse on the victim and on children – even once they have achieved safety – is severe and long-lasting. And families live with domestic abuse for too long before getting effective help – on average 2.6 years for high-risk abuse and three years for medium-risk. Given that many children living with domestic abuse are very young, the impact on them is severe.

At the point when a victim gets help, the abuse is likely to be escalating in either frequency or severity or both. Cutting the time it takes to find and help victims and their families is critical to stop murder, serious injury and enduring harm. As the cost per family where there is domestic abuse is £18,730, it is also expensive for the taxpayer.

Many victims do try to get help, but don't get the right help

It is not inevitable or acceptable that victims should try repeatedly to stop the abuse before they get the help they need. There are still far too many

missed opportunities to get help for families experiencing domestic abuse.

In the year before they got effective help:

⇨ Four in five high-risk victims (78%) and two-thirds of medium-risk victims (62%) reported the abuse to the police.

⇨ Nearly a quarter of high-risk victims (23%) and one in ten medium-risk victims went to an accident and emergency department because of their injuries. In the most extreme cases, victims reported that they attended A&E 15 times.

New SafeLives data shows that 85% of victims sought help five times on average from professionals in the year before they got effective help to stop the abuse. Regardless of whether the contact was about the abuse, each contact represents a chance for us to help the victim disclose and get help – a chance that was missed, leaving the family to live with abuse for longer.

How can we find families sooner?

All agencies must proactively identify families living with abuse

In recent years, an increasing number of victims and families have been identified by other agencies such as health and children's social services. But still too many families are only getting help when the abuse reaches crisis point and the police are called – and not every family gets the right help then.

Other professionals may also suspect that domestic violence is happening, but not know what to do

There are likely to be many more victims and families in contact with other statutory agencies, but they are not identified as living with domestic abuse. There is considerable potential in locating domestic abuse specialists in mainstream services, like hospitals. Programmes in GP surgeries and advice agencies have shown that it

is possible to significantly increase identification. And these programmes may also reach a group of victims and families who are different to – and in some cases, more vulnerable than – those identified by other routes.

Children and adult risk are not linked together – so we don't find and stop domestic abuse

Four in five of the families where a child is exposed to domestic abuse are known to at least one public agency. But too often agencies do not link up what they know about risks to each individual in a family, so other children or adults at risk of domestic abuse are not identified. Children's services must actively link the risks between mother and child in cases of domestic abuse. And agencies focused on adults – whether the victim or on the perpetrator – must make sure that they consider the risks to any children in the family.

Some victims of domestic abuse are not identified as readily

Particular groups of victims may be less visible to services or be given less priority. These include young people, victims from black, Asian and minority ethnic (BAME) backgrounds, male victims and LGBT victims. Services may miss victims who remain in a relationship with their abuser, a higher proportion of whom may be BAME. Some of this group may later leave the relationship, but effective help should be available to those victims at the point they seek it. Services may also not identify victims who do not have children living with them. Significant numbers of victims have high levels of complex or multiple needs related to mental health, drugs and alcohol: specialist mental health and substance misuse services should be proactive in identifying them.

Friends and family are often the first people to whom victims or children disclose abuse, but they may not know what to do

Although friends and family may be the first to know about abuse, they may not know how to get help. And if they do use local or national websites or helplines to seek support, these

may not be linked to local systems of support, so they might not get the right response.

Recommendations

We need to create the system to find every family as quickly as possible, and get the response right, first time, for every family.

⇨ All mainstream services should create an environment where any member of the family can tell someone about domestic abuse, and know that it will be acted on appropriately.

⇨ Services should make identifying domestic abuse part of their everyday practice.

⇨ There should be more specialist domestic abuse services based in the community – e.g. IDVA services in A&E.

⇨ Services should proactively seek out victims from diverse backgrounds – by locating support in the community for example.

⇨ We should judge the success of local domestic abuse strategies on whether they have cut the duration of domestic abuse.

⇨ There should be meaningful ways to seek help for individuals and for friends and family if they are worried about someone else.

⇨ Services must see and respond to the whole family – the child, the victim and the perpetrator.

⇨ Identifying abuse must result in action that helps the family become safe. And every area should have enough capacity to respond to every identified victim and family living with abuse.

⇨ SafeLives will investigate the potential of a One Front Door approach to increase identification.

⇨ The above information is reprinted with kind permission from SafeLives. Please visit www.safelives.org.uk for further information.

© SafeLives 2016

Only 4% of people using Clare's Law (Domestic Violence Disclosure Scheme) are men

Charity reveals significant underuse of the Domestic Violence Disclosure Scheme ('Clare's Law') by men.

Following Freedom of Information requests to police forces, the ManKind Initiative charity has revealed that of those (22) who could supply the data by gender, only one in 25 (4%) of requests to the Domestic Violence Disclosure Scheme (Clare's Law) were made by men. This is despite the fact that on average one in five (20%) victims of domestic abuse[1] who report to the same police forces are men, thereby proving that they do not believe the scheme is open to them.

The aim of the scheme (introduced in March 2014) is to provide anyone with a formal mechanism to make enquiries about their partner if they are worried that they may have been abusive in the past.

Research by the charity shows that between its introduction on 8 March 2014 and 5 January 2015, of those 22 police forces who could supply the data broken by gender, it was only used by 64 men (4%) and 1,547 women (96%). In five police forces no man had used the scheme (Staffordshire, Lincolnshire, Cambria, Cambridgeshire and Bedfordshire).

The charity raised concerns[2] in the 2011 government consultation that the over-use of the term 'Clare's Law' would lead to men thinking this scheme was not available to them. To address this, the charity wants local Police and Crime Commissioners to ensure that everyone in their area, including domestic abuse professionals, fully understand it is available for men to use as much as for women. All

publicity, information and training about the scheme is referred to as 'The Domestic Violence Disclosure Scheme', not just 'Clare's Law' and that both female and male victims are referred to.

Ian McNicholl[3], domestic abuse survivor and honorary patron of the ManKind Initiative, said:

"Had it been available to me, why would I have taken advantage of this scheme whilst I was been victimised if I thought it was just for women? It is similar to asking pensioners, 'Why are you not going on a Club 18-30 Holiday?' The clue is in the often-used title. This life-changing legislation is available to men right across England and Wales and they should be encouraged to come forward and seek help from the police. Don't be like me, please make the request to the police; alternatively, speak to friends and family and ask them to make the request on your behalf."

Mark Brooks, chairman of the ManKind Initiative, said:

"It is great news that so many women have used the scheme but given that so many men are also victims of domestic abuse as well, it is concerning that so few are asking for information. It is vital that men, family members, friends and neighbours are also aware they can use it, as the figures clearly show this needs to be addressed and can be done so with better publicity."

The Home Office reports that male victims (29%) are nearly twice as likely as women (17%) to not tell anyone about partner abuse. Only 10% of male victims will tell the police (27% women).

1 June 2015

⇨ The above information is reprinted with kind permission from the ManKind Initiative. Please visit www.mankindnews. wordpress.com for further information.

1 ManKind Initiative FOI responses on number of men and women reporting to police forces between January 2012 and June 2014: https://mankindnews.wordpress.com/2015/01/26/male-victims-police/

2 ManKind Initiative response to government consultation (2011) http://www.mankind.org.uk/pdfs/Mankind%20Clares%20Law%20response%20final.pdf

3 Ian McNicholl is a domestic abuse survivor. His partner was sentenced to seven years in prison in 2008. Since that time, Ian has campaigned across the UK to ensure the voices of male victims are heard and that services are provided.

© ManKind Initiative 2016

Domestic violence legislation in England and Wales: timeline

From curfews on wife beating to the creation of the first refuge: the landmark moments in the ongoing struggle to end domestic abuse.

1857 – Rule of Thumb

A judge reportedly states that a man may beat his wife so long as he uses "a rod not thicker than his thumb". Many people consider this to be common law throughout the 19th century.

1860 – Law of Coverture

At the point of marriage, a husband became legally responsible for the actions of both his wife and children. This meant he was entitled to use physical or verbal abuse to control their behaviour.

1870 – Married Women's Property Act

Before 1870, when a woman married, her property automatically became her husband's. After this act, any money she earned or inherited while married stayed hers.

1895 – Curfew on wife beating

This city of London byelaw made hitting your wife between the hours of 10pm and 7am illegal – because the noise was keeping people awake.

1923 – Matrimonial Causes Act

This act marked a big change in divorce law. Before, a wife had to prove her husband had been unfaithful and show evidence of other faults. After 1923, adultery could be a sole reason for divorce for women as well as men.

1956 – Sexual Offences Act

This was the first time rape was defined under specific criteria, such as incest, sex with a girl under 16, no consent, use of drugs, anal sex and impersonation.

1971 – First safe house

The charity Refuge opens the first safe house in Chiswick, west London, for women and children fleeing domestic abuse.

1976 – Domestic Violence and Matrimonial Proceedings Act

This was the first legislation dedicated to combating domestic violence. It gave survivors new rights by offering civil protection orders (injunctions) for those at risk of abuse.

1977 – Housing Act (Homeless Persons) 1977

Women and children at risk of violence were acknowledged as homeless. This meant they gained the right to state-funded temporary accommodation.

1991 – Marital rape criminalised

Before 1991 it was a husband's legal right to rape his wife – marriage implied consent for sexual intercourse. This was the first time a woman had legal protection from marital rape.

2003 – Inter-ministerial group on domestic violence is established

This group received crucial evidence on the scale of domestic violence and use of refuges. Women's Aid (a charity dedicated to ending domestic violence) played a significant role in providing testimony.

2004 – Domestic Violence, Crime and Victims Act

This made common assault an arrestable offence. This meant that police could arrest a suspect immediately, rather than leaving them with someone vulnerable while they applied for a warrant.

2010 – Government strategy is set out to end violence against women and girls

The strategy developed a 2011 plan which included financial commitments to support rape crisis centres and specialist training for health workers in the treatment of survivors.

2014 – Clare's Law

A law is implemented across England and Wales giving people the right to ask police about a partner's history of domestic abuse.

The above information is reprinted with kind permission from *The Guardian*. Please visit www.theguardian.com for further information.

One in three people do not know domestic abuse can happen after a relationship has ended

By Rachel Moss

You do not have to be in a relationship with a physically, emotionally or financially abusive person to be a victim of domestic abuse.

But new figures from Citizens Advice reveal that one in three people do not know that domestic abuse can happen between former partners.

The research also shows victims can be at greater risk of being harmed after leaving an abusive relationship, but many people are unaware that domestic abuse can continue when victims are no longer living with the perpetrator.

Our lack of knowledge may mean we're missing signs that suggest a friend or family member needs help.

The survey of over 2,000 British adults found that just one in five (22%) think it is always easy to tell what counts as domestic abuse.

A total of 13% believe domestic abuse can only be between two people in a relationship who live together, not among those who are casually dating.

Abuse that occurs after a relationship has ended often includes a financial or psychological element, but the report revealed that our knowledge in this area is seriously lacking.

Speaking to HuffPost UK Lifestyle, director of policy at Women's Aid Hilary Fisher said it is "deeply concerning that domestic abuse is not always recognised for what it is".

"It means that women are less likely to receive the support they need to move past their abuse. We need a huge cultural change around understanding what domestic violence is," she added.

Last year, the Citizens Advice report *Controlling Money, Controlling Lives* revealed that victims of financial abuse had access to their bank accounts restricted, were stolen from and had their property destroyed.

Some victims sought help after being left with huge debts when they were forced to take out loans for their abuser. The financial abuse was in some cases accompanied by intimidation, physical violence and repeated death threats.

An analysis of almost 200 cases of financial abuse brought to local Citizens Advice between January and June last year revealed that nine in ten victims were women.

However, the new research showed that people are more than twice as likely to know that domestic abuse can include a psychological element than a financial one.

Only two in five (39%) are aware of the financial side of abuse compared to four in five (86%) who are aware of the psychological side.

On top of that, two in five people (39%) are not aware making a partner account for all their spending can constitute domestic abuse.

"The suffering of domestic abuse victims is going undetected. Many people do not realise abuse can occur after a relationship has ended and be financial or psychological, as well as physical," Gillian Guy, chief executive of Citizens Advice, said in a statement.

"Without the knowledge and understanding of the extent of abuse it is difficult for family and friends to make sure people get the help they need.

CPS domestic violence prosecutions and convictions			
Year	Total prosecutions	Total convictions	Convictions as % of prosecutions
2008/09	67,094	48,465	72.2
2009/10	74,113	53,347	72.0
2010/11	82,187	59,101	71.9
2011/12	79,268	58,138	73.3
2012/13	70,702	52,549	74.3
2013/14	78,071	58,276	74.6
2014/15	92,779	68,601	73.9

Source: Domestic violence in England and Wales, Briefing Paper, John Woodhouse and Noel Dempsey, House of Commons Library, 26 February 2016. Licensed under the Open Parliament Licence v3.0. Visit www.parliament.uk for further information.

"New measures from the Government to make coercive control illegal will ensure those found guilty of these crimes are punished. For this to truly help victims the public and authorities need support to identify abuse."

Citizens Advice is currently developing new guidance that will aim to better equip everyone, from friends and family through to professionals, to identify all forms of abuse and take the right steps to help victims get the support they need.

For support on domestic violence here in the UK, you can contact Women's Aid – support for abused women and children – or call the National Domestic Violence Helpline, run by Women's Aid and Refuge, on 0808 2000 247. Contact Broken Rainbow – the LGBT domestic violence charity – on 0845 2 60 55 60. Or contact Men's Advice Line – advice and support for men experiencing domestic violence and abuse – on 0808 801 0327.

2 July 2015

⇨ The above information is reprinted with kind permission from The Huffington Post UK. Please visit www.huffingtonpost.co.uk for further information.

False accusations preventing men from reporting domestic abuse – study finds

Male victims of domestic violence are reluctant to report the abuse they suffer for fear of being accused of violence themselves, according to new research by a Teesside University academic.

Dr Jessica McCarrick, a Senior Lecturer in Counselling Psychology and Chartered Psychologist, says that men are often arrested under false accusations and their disclosures of victimisation are initially dismissed.

She is calling for more to be done to support male victims of intimate partner violence – encouraging men to report abuse and feel assured they will be taken seriously.

Dr McCarrick has carried out interviews with male victims who say that, as well as the trauma of domestic abuse, their negative experiences are perpetuated within the criminal justice system by being treated like the guilty party or feeling dismissed by the police.

The number of women convicted of perpetrating domestic abuse has more than quadrupled in the past ten years from 806 in 2004/05, to 3,735 in 2013/14.

Statistics show that an average of one third of domestic abuse victims are male.

One man, who did not want to be named, said he was arrested on three separate occasions following false counter allegations from his wife.

He said: "In the latest incident I made the initial complaint to police as my wife assaulted me. But when they arrived, they showed little concern and instead arrested me because my wife made a counter allegation. I certainly feel that more compassion and empathy needs to be shown towards male victims of domestic violence."

Dr McCarrick, who works within Teesside University's School of Social Sciences, Business & Law, says that this type of account is not at all uncommon.

"Within my research, the predominant experience is of men being arrested under false charges and their disclosures of being the victim are not taken seriously, despite having evidence.

"Men find it incredibly difficult to talk about their experiences of domestic violence because of the shame and emasculation they feel is associated with it. To find the courage to speak out, only to be accused of violence themselves, is incredibly disheartening and ultimately prevents countless men from reporting intimate partner violence."

Dr McCarrick is calling for more understanding of the emotional experiences of men and encouraging a more balanced, gender-informed perspective of domestic violence.

"When there was a positive experience of a police member, one who offered advice about support services for example, this appeared to reduce the negative psychological impact of being arrested under false charges."

Intimate partner violence should be viewed as a human issue rather than a gender issue, argues Dr McCarrick and there should be more services and support to enable men to seek the help and sanctuary they desperately require.

She added: "Campaigners and researchers made waves in the 1970's, which had a positive impact and improved service provision for women – it is time to do the same for men.

"Promoting awareness of the plight of male survivors may encourage men to report abuse and feel assured that they will be taken seriously.

"Intimate partner violence is an issue which affects men and women within both heterosexual and homosexual relationships and I would like to see increased funding to improve service provision and development in order to support all people affected by this issue."

⇨ The above information is reprinted with kind permission from Teesside University. Please visit www.tees.ac.uk for further information.

working for decades now to dispel the myth that domestic violence equals physical and sexual violence. Women often report, as they did in our pilot study, that it wasn't always the physical violence that was the worst. It was the more subtle forms of control. It was not having their own money, seeing their children or their pets being treated badly and having to restrict their lives in an attempt to live by their partner's rules to keep them happy.

This is why we included six different measures of success in our research. The other five measures of success – respectful relationships; expanded space for action; decreased isolation; enhanced parenting and understanding the impact of domestic violence – did all see improvements as well, though not to the extent that was seen for the physical and sexual violence, and in many cases not to the extent that women might have hoped for.

Fewer children were scared of the perpetrator, fewer children were worried about the safety of their mother, men were less likely to try to make excuses for their behaviour and less likely to try to prevent women from contacting their friend. But this kind of behaviour did still continue for a significant proportion of men.

Perpetrator programmes can allow men who are ready to choose to stop using violence and abuse in relationships to take steps towards change. Sometimes these will be tiny steps, sometimes they will be great leaps. For most of the women and children in our research, lives were improved to some degree.

Can a leopard change its spots? No, because a leopard is born with spots, it does not make the choice to continue to have them. Men are not born violent, they derive benefits from not being held accountable for their use of violence and abuse, and just as they make decisions about other areas of their lives, they can choose to stop being violent and abusive. Perpetrator programmes can help them make those changes.

13 January 2015

⇨ The above information is reprinted with kind permission from *The Conversation*. Please visit www.theconversation. com for further information.

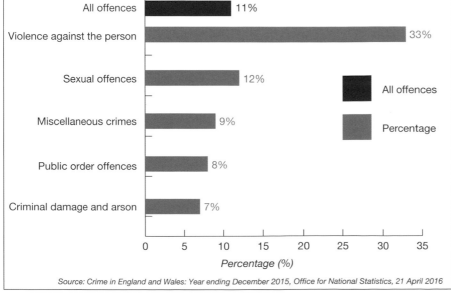

Proportion of offences recorded by the police in England and Wales which were flagged as domestic abuse related, selected offence groups, April to December 2015

Offence group	Percentage
All offences	11%
Violence against the person	33%
Sexual offences	12%
Miscellaneous crimes	9%
Public order offences	8%
Criminal damage and arson	7%

Source: Crime in England and Wales: Year ending December 2015, Office for National Statistics, 21 April 2016

British Muslim women's helpline: their voices won't go unheard again

Today [14 January 2015] sees the launch of the first national helpline for Muslim women and girls, tackling problems such as sexual abuse, forced marriage and divorce – still taboo subjects in their communities. Alia Waheed speaks to the people behind it.

By Alia Waheed

When the Muslim Women's Network (MWNUK) launched a report, last year, on sexual exploitation in the Asian community, it could only have dreamed that something like this would come to pass.

That report was called *Unheard Voices – The Sexual Exploitation of Asian Girls and Young Women*. Its publication coincided with the revelations around child sexual exploitation by Asian gangs in Rotherham and challenged the view that the issue was purely one of race and that somehow, Asian girls were left untouched by abusers because of loyalties to their own culture.

MWNUK found that a worrying number of women and girls were slipping through the net, as agencies – such as social services and the police – grappled with the difficulties reaching out to victims because of cultural sensitivities – those same points of faith, which are exploited by their abusers to ensure their victims' silence.

It confirmed what many already knew – that many Muslim girls and women are trapped in a cycle of abuse and violence because of a lack of services. What's more, it recommended a helpline be set up as an outlet for them to confide their problems and seek advice.

And today, as a result of the charity's awareness-raising activities, the first national helpline for Muslim women is being launched by Minister for Women and Equalities, Jo Swinson.

The helpline will initially be run part time by trained, bilingual staff and will be accompanied by a website containing information on the issues which they are most commonly asked about: sexual abuse, domestic violence and divorce.

Its aim? To make sure the voices of Muslim girls and women never go unheard again.

Sadly, it's impossible to know just how many are suffering right now. Figures for violence against women in the Muslim community remain elusive.

Last year, the Home Office Forced Marriage Unit was informed of 1,302 cases. Of these, 15 per cent of victims were under 15, though figures peaked in the 16 to 17 age group, coinciding with the age that young women finish school. While the Iranian and Kurdish Women's Rights Organisation found, under the Freedom of Information Act, that more than 2,800 incidents of 'honour'-based violence were reported to police across the UK in 2010.

Within four months of its report last year, MWNUK had received 35 case studies from different agencies – a surprising number from what is traditionally such a closed community and especially considering the intimidation victims often face from their abusers, in the name of 'family honour'. It suggests that the real number is much higher.

Among them was a young woman, raped by 30 men, including a father and his schoolboy son, during a horrific six-hour attack. The common factor in each case? That cultural and religious issues were perpetuating the abuse and preventing victims from accessing help.

The desperate need for a helpline was cemented by the growing number of calls MWNUK staff were receiving from desperate women.

"We are predominantly a campaigning organisation but found we were getting many helpline-type enquiries," said Shaista Gohir MBE, Chair of MWNUK.

"These calls confirmed that there's definitely a gap in services for Muslim women, which are faith and culturally sensitive, and non-judgemental. While there are services for specific issues such as domestic violence, there hasn't been a general helpline."

The charity also found many women were struggling to reconcile their faith with their problems. They simply couldn't find an alternative perspective to those patriarchal interpretations – which so often dominate religious discourse – that had been used against them.

"More women are asking about the religious implications of issues like abortion," explains Shaista "Often they feel that Islam cannot be as harsh as they've been led to believe. We can understand that predicament.

"We don't pretend to be religious scholars, or force our beliefs upon them. We give them a range of religious perspectives and show them that their faith does make allowances."

MWNUK began as an advisory group to the Government on issues relating to Muslim women and public policy in 2003, before becoming an independent organisation four years later.

The Birmingham-based charity now consists of a network of nearly 700 individuals and organisations, and has become one of the leading campaigning voices for Muslim women in the UK.

The power of that collective voice led to 19-year-old Shabana* contacting the charity after the attempted rape of her sister, then 11, by their uncle.

"Our dad left when we were small and mum had health problems so her family helped a lot," she explains. "But as we got older, we grew aware of how controlling my uncle was and how my mum and her sisters were scared of him. They had to ask for permission every time they went somewhere.

"Once I went with my grandmother to stay with cousins, while their mum was in hospital. When my uncle found out, he told my mum to bring me home or he would kill her and burn the house down."

It was while her grandmother was in Pakistan, that their uncle began bombarding Shabana with calls, trying to lure her to her gran's empty flat.

"He claimed he had pictures of me with boys and wanted to meet at the flat to discuss them, or he'd tell my mum.

"Every time he texted me to meet up I'd swear at him. But he'd always reply back that he loved me. I threatened to call the police, but he told me to go ahead because my mum wasn't going to believe me over him.

"I knew this was true, so I never told anyone."

A few weeks later, while Shabana was at a driving lesson, their uncle turned up at the family home and offered to take her 11-year-old sister shopping. Instead he took the terrified youngster to their grandmother's flat and tried to rape her.

"When I got home, she started crying and said 'it's uncle, he kissed me, touched me and make me do things'. I screamed the house down and phoned the police. Even then, my mum told me to stop so we could deal with it within the family. But I knew they just wanted to talk me out of it."

Shabana's uncle was arrested, but as the trial date got nearer, the pressure on her to withdraw the case grew.

"Our whole family was against us. They went on about family honour, playing the religious card to make us feel guilty and accused my sister of leading him on."

It was at this point that Shabana came across an article on MWNUK and contacted them. They were able to support the girls and raise awareness about their case.

"MWNUK understand about our culture and how, when things like this happen within Muslim families, the first reaction is to keep quiet and make sure nobody finds out. But the charity are completely against that. Knowing we weren't alone gave us the strength to carry on."

Their uncle pleaded guilty to assault and oral rape and was sentenced to 64 months in prison in June.

Shabana added: "A helpline is needed because many Muslim women don't have anybody to turn to. It's not talked about in our communities."

One of the most recent cases the MWNUK dealt with concerned a 17-year-old victim of forced marriage. Aisha* faced months of emotional and physical abuse by her parents before she was taken to Pakistan to wed her 30-year-old cousin, who she'd never even met.

"It started off with lectures about family honour, but then they started beating me with leather belts. They took away my phone, purse and Western clothes. I wasn't allowed

to see my friends or go to the shop unaccompanied," she explained.

When Aisha arrived in Pakistan, she was warned that if she didn't play the role of the happy bride, she would die.

"With my dad, it wasn't about family honour, but his honour. He threatened to kill me if I didn't go through with it. I knew he meant it.

"On the wedding night, I told my husband that I didn't want to sleep with him, so he forced me. He raped me three or four times each night. Then, in the morning, I had to pretend I was happy.

"When I came back to England, my parents thought I was happy, so they let me have my phone back. When everyone was asleep, I looked up forced marriages and found MWNUK.

"I told them what had happened. They calmed me down and advised me. One night, I ran away with nothing. MWNUK helped me find accommodation, food and clothes. They also assisted me in getting a legal and Islamic divorce. It's changed my life."

With the launch of the first national helpline for Muslim women and girls helpline, voices of women such as Aisha and Shabana will no longer remain unheard. The charity hope that more will find the confidence to come forward and seek help.

Perhaps, finally, the veil of silence which has kept these problems hidden for so long, will finally be lifted.

*Names and identifying details have been changed to protect the women's identities.

The Muslim Women's Network Helpline can be contacted on 0800 999 5786 or you can visit their website: www.mwnhelpline.co.uk.

14 January 2015

⇨ The above information is reprinted with kind permission from *The Telegraph*. Please visit www.telegraph.co.uk for further information.

Helping parents suffering at the hands of children

Last year, West Midlands Police dealt with more than 17,000 domestic abuse related crimes.

Among those who turned to the force's specialist Public Protection Unit for help breaking free from behind-closed-doors abuse was a woman who'd been assaulted – kicked, punched, throttled and spat at – on an almost daily basis.

It was an awful catalogue of abuse stretching back several years. And even more shocking when she disclosed the offender was not a violent partner... but her 12-year-old daughter.

Child-on-parent abuse was thrust into the spotlight this summer courtesy of a *Coronation Street* storyline in which Leanne Battersby suffered at the hands of her 12-year-old stepson Simon.

What started with sullen stares quickly escalated to unruly behaviour, verbal abuse and, ultimately, physical assaults ... and left Leanne toying over how to deal with the tearaway and whether to call in outside help.

But such episodes aren't the preserve of soap opera fiction.

It's estimated that one in ten parents have experienced violent outbursts from a child, while national helplines are taking around 11,000 calls a year from parents being abused and seeking support to control children.

Last year (April '14 to March '15) West Midlands Police received 460 reports of under-18s committing domestic offences. Of those, 194 were child-on-parent offences, including 115 physical assaults, plus threats to kill, criminal damage, domestic thefts and fraud.

The youngest offender was a 12-year-old girl from Coventry whose mum called police to report being at breaking point following repeated attacks that started when her daughter was aged just eight.

She was arrested on suspicion of assault in January this year but, following enquiries by Public Protection officers who are specially trained to deal sensitively with such cases, the woman chose not to make a complaint and the case was filed.

The case is now managed by children's services; the girl is being supported by child mental health specialists (CAMHS) to manage anger issues, while other children in the family have allocated social workers.

Public Protection Inspector Sally Simpson said: "Incidents range from humiliating language and threats, belittling a parent and damage to property, to stealing from the home or bouts of explosive violence. And the outbursts, usually in the home, can be sparked by the smallest of incidents.

"Around six in ten such allegations passed to us are dropped because the victim decides not to support a formal prosecution. Understandably, most are reluctant to criminalise their own children and will exhaust all other options to address the issue, and try to change their child's behaviour, before resorting to a formal prosecution.

"They are challenging cases to investigate ... and with repeat offenders the focus has to be on repairing a fractured family. We have to ask whether taking a child to court or blighting them with a police caution is in their best interests and will address underlying issues. Probably not ... and if anything it can make matters worse."

Of the 194 under-18 child-on-parent crime reports received by West Midlands Police last year only 13 progressed to a formal charge, ten teenagers were given youth cautions, and 12 complaints were dealt with through community resolutions.

Detective Inspector Simpson, added: "We've come a long way in just a few years because previously there may have been a temptation to lock a young offender in a police cell to 'teach them a lesson'.

"We do still get parents calling us in the hope police presence will act as a warning shot – and in some cases it helps – but we now have a holistic approach that involves working with agencies like child mental health (CAMHS) and education providers. Aggressive and conforming behaviours are learnt so working with partners to change mind-sets and behaviours is essential.

"Each case is different – but if there are genuine concerns for the parents' safety we would intervene and remove the child. It's always a balancing act."

Other recent cases dealt with by the force's Public Protection Units include a Birmingham mum punched in the face by her 15-year-old son when she asked him to help around the house, and a 15-year-old from Wolverhampton who hurled an ashtray through a TV screen during an argument.

Neither parent wanted police to pursue a criminal investigation – but DI Simpson said it's important domestic abuse sufferers contact police for support and guidance rather than suffer in silence.

She added: "Statistics show we've recorded almost 200 under-18 child-on-parent domestic crimes in 12 months ... but I don't think there's any doubt it's an under-reported offence and I suspect the actual figure is much higher.

"Survivors tell us they'd been reluctant to contact police out of embarrassment, a feeling it would be admitting failing as a parent, or a general unconditional love for their children. And sometimes there may be autism or other behavioural issues triggering outbursts that need to be taken into account.

"Another question parents are left asking themselves is how much rebelliousness they are expected to take as part of the growing-up process. This is purely subjective – but if lashing out at parental restrictions, or losing sight of boundaries, manifests itself in repeated aggression then I'd encourage parents to contact us.

"In the short term we can protect people and property. But we can also start the process with children's services, education, mental health or probation to ensure we have a clear understanding of the family history and develop a plan to best address a child's behaviour."

West Midlands Police recently doubled the number of officers in its Public Protection Unit – meaning one in ten of all officers now work in these specialist teams – and now has dedicated domestic abuse teams to investigate crimes, protect victims and manage offenders.

Detective Superintendent Angie Whitaker, force lead for domestic abuse, said: "A report by HMIC in March found West Midlands Police provides a good service when identifying and tackling domestic abuse – commending our investment in this area and the positive shift of culture across the force.

"These specialist units have all the knowledge and tactics they need to protect people from harm and I would urge all domestic abuse victims to speak out; they will be listened to, taken seriously and their report will be investigated fully."

To speak to your local Public Protection Unit call West Midlands Police on 101. More support is available through:

www.youngminds.org.uk – a child mental health charity and parent helpline

www.rosalieryriefoundation.org.uk – behavioural management specialising in domestic abuse and destructive relationships within families

2 October 2015

⇨ The above information is reprinted with kind permission from the West Midlands Police. Please visit www.west-midlands.police.uk for further information.

Closure of refuges could send UK back to *Cathy Come Home* days

By Lydia Smith

Domestic violence refuges are essential for safeguarding the lives of women and children against abuse. But as they close one by one, the network is under terrible strain. As local funding is cut, the country is entering a crisis that could set support for some of the most vulnerable back by four decades.

Born out of the feminist movement of the 1970s, Britain was one of the first countries to pioneer special safe houses for women fleeing physical and sexual violence at home. The first of its kind, Chiswick's Women's Aid for battered women was opened in London in 1971 by Erin Pizzey.

But today [25 November], on the International Day for the Elimination of Violence against Women, Women's Aid estimates 155 women and 103 children are turned away from the refuges that still exist.

According to Sandra Horley, chief executive of the national domestic violence charity Refuge, the closures pose the possibility of "returning to the days of *Cathy Come Home*".

Several reasons underpin why refuges are struggling, in scenes reminiscent of the 1966 BBC television play. In some areas, safe houses face closure in favour of preventative work and support in the community but many are shut with no alternative for victims of domestic violence.

Funding cuts

Other houses have had funding cut because they do not take men, while some have been shut entirely without alternative accommodation being provided. The Haven Wolverhampton, which has run refuges for 41 years, recently had its funding cut by £300,000 and is struggling to maintain services. It has been forced to reserve some of its places for men, even though it has not had a male referral so far.

Sandra Horley, chief executive of the national domestic violence charity Refuge, tells IBTimes UK refuge provision is under threat as a result of ongoing cuts to local funding and poor commissioning practices.

"Over the last few years, local authority funding for domestic violence services has been eroded as a result of ongoing austerity measures," she said. "Services for black and minority ethnic women have been hit particularly hard. Refuge has also seen the emergence of a number of worrying trends in commissioning practices."

Such commissioning practices include limiting numbers of non-local women able to stay in refuges.

"Some commissioners are demanding that refuge spaces be reserved for women from the local area," Horley adds. "This demonstrates a very poor understanding of the reality of domestic violence, which often forces women and children to flee across local boundaries in order to stay safe.

"Some contracts do not include any refuge provision at all, whilst others are replacing refuges with dispersed accommodation. This means that abused women and children are housed in isolated units, with little support to help them recover from the trauma of experiencing horrific, and often prolonged, abuse."

Refuge is currently calling on the Government to open a public inquiry into the failure of state agencies to protect women and children experiencing domestic abuse.

Cathy Come Home

Some commissioners are imposing restrictions on the length of time women and children are able to stay in a refuge, threatening the security of women who have uprooted their lives to escape violence.

Although the Government has this week committed to a £10 million national fund for refuges, women's rights groups have said it is vital this fund is matched with a commitment to exploring a new model of funding for refuges that supports them in the long term.

"We are in real danger of returning to the days of *Cathy Come Home*," Horley says. "Without adequate refuge provision, women experiencing domestic violence will be faced with a stark choice: flee to live rough on the streets with their children, or remain with their abuser and risk further violence – or worse."

Refuge contracts have encouraged women to move on after just weeks or days. According to Refuge statistics, 55% of women accessing the charity's safe houses had experienced threats to kill, and another 55% had been strangled or choked by their abuser. It is commonly known, yet nonetheless distressing, that two women a week are killed as a result of domestic violence.

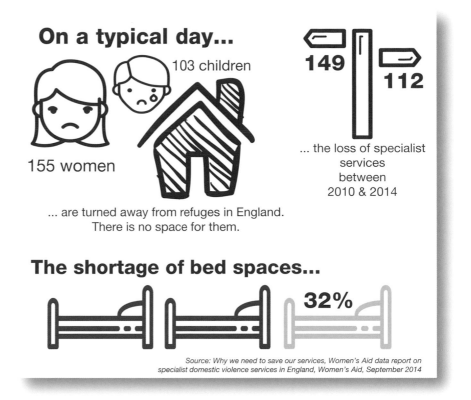

On a typical day...

103 children
155 women

... are turned away from refuges in England. There is no space for them.

149 | 112

... the loss of specialist services between 2010 & 2014

The shortage of bed spaces...

32%

Source: Why we need to save our services, Women's Aid data report on specialist domestic violence services in England, Women's Aid, September 2014

"Empowering women and children to overcome trauma and rebuild their lives is highly specialist, intensive work – it takes a lot longer than just a few weeks," Horley adds.

"Refuges are so much more than just a roof over a head. Behind the walls of these houses, lives are transformed – our specialist refuge workers support women and children to rebuild every aspect of their lives, from helping them to stay safe, access health services, legal advocacy and immigration advice, and get back into work or education."

Isolation is another problem that refuges seek to tackle. Abused women and children are often isolated by their perpetrators, who deliberately cut off contact from friends or family to exert dominance and control.

"When women come to a refuge, they are able to share their experiences with other women who understand what they have been through. They realise – often for the first time – that they are not alone, and that they are not to blame for the abuse. Refuges facilitate this powerful recovery process," Horley says.

"Put quite simply, these services save lives."

25 November 2014

⇨ The above information is reprinted with kind permission from the *International Business Times*. Please visit www.ibtimes.co.uk for further information.

First domestic violence safe house opens for women over 45 (and about time too)

The country's first safe house for domestic violence victims over the age of 45 has opened.

Eva Women's Aid, based in Redcar, Teesside – which has worked with victims aged up to 80 – has opened the specialist home for older people because they have different needs.

"This dedicated safe house, with fully-trained staff on hand, will enable us to help them turn their lives around and break the cycle of abuse"

Older women are less likely to report maltreatment by their partner, the organisation said. It said it had found that if they were accommodated with younger victims, they would 'mother' them to the detriment of their own needs.

The charity, based in Redcar's High Street, already operates two safe houses in the Teesside area geared towards young women.

The new residence will offer temporary housing for up to four women at a time and the first residents have moved in.

Chief executive Richinda Taylor said: "Women over 45 have different needs to younger victims and we have found that when they are housed together, the older women tend to take on a maternal role.

"This can be at the cost of their own personal needs and we want to ensure that they're not overlooked.

"We've worked with women aged 80 and over who've been subjected to violence and psychological control all of their adult lives and sadly many women believe that there's no way out for them.

"This dedicated safe house, with fully-trained staff on hand, will enable us to help them turn their lives around and break the cycle of abuse."

The scheme has been supported by the Charity Bank organisation with a £55,000 loan.

Alistair Jenkins, its North East manager, said: "Eva's innovative approach and expertise supporting domestic abuse victims is being shared with other organisations working in the field so that similar schemes aimed at women over 45 can be opened across the UK."

1 June 2015

⇨ The above information is reprinted with kind permission from the Press Association. Please visit www.pressassociation.com for further information.

© Press Association 2016

Why are there no refuges for male victims of domestic violence?

According to a 2005 study, 15% of women and 6% of men in Ireland suffer some form of domestic violence. Yet none of the shelters in the country provide beds for men:

"There is not one bed for men suffering from domestic violence," said Niamh Farrell of AMEN, the only domestic violence resource in Ireland for men.

"If there is no bed for men there is no bed for the children [with the men]," she said, explaining that fathers or guardians may not want to leave their children in the domestic situation.

"You can encourage them to look for help but in terms of housing, we can't do anything to help them with that because there is no refuge."

This is ridiculous. Abused men face the same problems as abused women. They need to find a safe place for themselves and sometimes their children. If no-one provides them with safe housing, many abused men end up in homeless shelters and on the streets. This proves risky because some shelters will not accept men with children, and obviously living on the streets with a child is a poor option. That leaves two options: remain in the abusive situation or leave the situation yourself, but leave the children with the abuser.

Both are untenable, yet little is done to help abused men seeking shelter. Many abused men assume that they have access to equal services:

"[They] will ring and assume that there are the same services for men and women, they ask 'where do I go?', 'but there's one for women, there should be one for men'. They just think there should be same services for men as there are for women."

There should be. There is no excuse for not providing men with the same support given to women. The argument that women are in greater need of help falls flat. The majority of victims of violence are male, yet no hospital turns away women because they see more men.

This is not how one runs a support service. One should provide access for everyone because one never knows when it is needed. It is particularly important in this situation because so few abused men come forward. Perhaps we will find that there are more abused men than we think if we open the doors to them.

7 July 2014

⇨ The above information is reprinted with kind permission from Toy Soldiers. Please visit toysoldier. wordpress.com for further information.

© Toy Soldiers 2016

How does the Government define domestic violence?

In March 2013, the Home Office introduced an extended definition of domestic violence and abuse to be used across government. The definition includes young people aged 16 to 17 and coercive or controlling behaviour. It is hoped that extending the definition in this way will raise awareness that young people can be victims of domestic violence and that they will come forward and get the support they need.

The definition of domestic violence and abuse is:

Any incident or pattern of incidents of controlling, coercive or threatening behaviour, violence or abuse between those aged 16 or over who are or have been intimate partners or family members regardless of gender or sexuality. This can encompass, but is not limited to, the following types of abuse:

- psychological
- physical
- sexual
- financial
- emotional

Controlling behaviour

Controlling behaviour is a range of acts designed to make a person subordinate and/or dependent by isolating them from sources of support, exploiting their resources and capacities for personal gain, depriving them of the means needed for independence, resistance and escape and regulating their everyday behaviour.

Coercive behaviour

Coercive behaviour is an act or a pattern of acts of assault, threats, humiliation and intimidation or other abuse that is used to harm, punish, or frighten their victim.

Source: Domestic violence in England and Wales, Briefing Paper, John Woodhouse and Noel Dempsey, House of Commons Library, 26 February 2016.

Licensed under the Open Parliament Licence v3.0. Visit www. parliament.uk for further information.

Key facts

- Two women are killed every week in England and Wales by a current or former partner (Office of National Statistics, 2015) – one woman killed every three days. (page 1)

- One in four women in England and Wales will experience domestic violence in their lifetimes and 8% will suffer domestic violence in any given year (Crime Survey of England and Wales, 2013/14). (page 1)

- 30% of domestic violence either starts or will intensify during pregnancy (Department of Health report, October 2004). (page 1)

- In 90% of domestic violence incidents in family households, children were in the same or the next room (Hughes, 1992). (page 1)

- 12.2% of men state they have been a victim of domestic abuse since they were 16. For every three victims of domestic abuse, two will be female and one will be male. (page 1)

- 4% of men and 8.2% of women were estimated to have experienced domestic abuse in 2014/15, equivalent to an estimated 600,000 male victims and 1.3 million female victims. (page 1)

- The British Crime Survey suggests that women are at greater risk of repeat victimisation and serious injury; 89% of those suffering four or more incidents are women. (page 2)

- 97% of women who contacted Rape Crisis said they knew the person who raped them. 43% of girls questioned in a national survey said the person responsible for an unwanted sexual experience was a boy they knew or were friends with. (page 4)

- Every year one million women experience at least one incident of domestic abuse – nearly 20,000 women a week. (page 5)

- One in five UK adults is a victim of financial abuse in a relationship. (page 7)

- Half of victims experience a partner taking financial assets without permission. (page 7)

- For women, financial abuse rarely happens in isolation – 86 per cent experience other forms of abuse. (page 7)

- A third of women worldwide have experienced physical or sexual violence at the hands of a partner, according to the first comprehensive research of its kind. (page 11)

- National surveys conducted in predominantly high-income countries find wide variation in rates of abuse in the preceding 12 months among adults aged over 60 years, ranging from 0.8% in Spain and 2.6% in the United Kingdom to upwards of 18% in Israel, 23.8% in Austria and 32% in Belgium. (page 15)

- In a survey by pet fostering charity Paws for Kids:

  - 66% said their abuser had threatened to harm their pets

  - 94% said if there had been a pet fostering service it would have made it easier for them to leave the violence, and so spare themselves and their children more abuse. (page 21)

- 1.1 million women and 720,000 men reported domestic violence in the past year. (page 23)

- Four in five high-risk victims (78%) and two-thirds of medium-risk victims (62%) reported the abuse to the police. (page 25)

- Nearly a quarter of high-risk victims (23%) and one in ten medium-risk victims went to an accident and emergency department because of their injuries. In the most extreme cases, victims reported that they attended A&E 15 times. (page 25)

- Research shows that between the introduction of Clare's Law on 8 March 2014 and 5 January 2015, of those 22 police forces who could supply the data broken by gender, it was only used by 64 men (4%) and 1,547 women (96%). In five police forces no man had used the scheme (Staffordshire, Lincolnshire, Cambria, Cambridgeshire and Bedfordshire). (page 26)

- When the public was asked whether there were any reasons they wouldn't tell somebody if they were worried about abuse, only 16% said nothing would stop them. (page 30)

- Last year, West Midlands Police dealt with more than 17,000 domestic abuse related crimes. (page 35)

- It's estimated that one in ten parents have experienced violent outbursts from a child, while national helplines are taking around 11,000 calls a year from parents being abused and seeking support to control children. (page 35)

- On a typical day, 103 children and 155 women are turned away from refuges in England because there is no space for them. (page 37)

Clare's Law

Also known as the Domestic Violence Disclosure Scheme, Clare's Law allows people to find out whether someone has a record of abusive offences, or if there is any other information that indicates they may be a risk.

Coercive control

The term coercive control refers to the aspects of domestic violence that encompass more than just physical abuse, e.g. psychological behaviour that removes a victim's freedom.

Domestic abuse/violence

Any incident of physical, sexual, emotional or financial abuse that takes place within an intimate partner relationship. Domestic abuse can be perpetrated by a spouse, partner or other family member and occurs regardless of gender, sex, race, class or religion.

Elder abuse

The abuse of elderly people.

Emotional abuse

Emotional abuse refers to a victim being verbally attacked, criticised and put down. Following frequent exposure to this abuse, the victim's mental wellbeing suffers as their self-esteem is destroyed and the perpetrator's control over them increases. They may suffer from feelings of worthlessness, believing that they deserve the abuse or that if they were to leave the abuser they would never find another partner. A victim way also have been convinced by their abuser that the abuse is their fault. The abuser can use these feelings to manipulate the victim.

Financial abuse

Financial, or economic, abuse involves controlling the victim's finances. This limits the victim's independence and ability to access help, and restricts their ability to leave the abusive relationship. Financial abuse can include withholding money or credit cards, exploiting mutual assets and forcing someone to quit their job or work against their will.

Female genital mutilation (FGM)

FGM is a non-medical cultural practice that involves partially or totally removing a girl or woman's external genitalia.

Forced marriage

A marriage that takes place without the consent of one or both parties. Forced marriage is not the same as arranged marriage, which is organised by family or friends but which both parties freely enter into.

Gaslighting

Psychologically manipulating someone by making them believe their behaviour is at fault.

Honour crime

An 'honour' crime or killing occurs when family members take action against a relative who is thought to have brought shame on the family. The victims are mostly women who are accused of dishonouring their family by going against their wishes (for example, by fleeing a forced marriage).

Perpetrator programme

A rehabilitation programme for perpetrators of domestic abuse which aims to help them understand and try to change their abusive behaviour.

Physical abuse

Physical abuse involves the use of violence or force against a victim and can including hitting, slapping, kicking, pushing, strangling or other forms of violence. Physical assault is a crime and the police have the power to protect victims, but in a domestic violence situation it can sometimes take a long time for the violence to come to light. Some victims are too afraid to go to the police, believe they can reform the abuser (who they may still love) or have normalised their abusive situation and do not realise they can get help.

Refuge

A shelter or safe house, offering a safe place for victims of domestic violence and their children to stay. Refuges can provide practical advice as well as emotional support for victims of domestic abuse until they can find somewhere more permanent to stay.

Revenge porn

Revenge porn refers to distributing or making public explicit images or videos of a former partner.

Sexual abuse

Sexual abuse occurs when a victim is forced into a sexual act against their will, through violence or intimidation. This can include rape. Sexual abuse is always a crime, no matter what the relationship is between the victim and perpetrator.

Stalking

Repeatedly following, watching or harassing someone. Stalking usually takes place over a long period of time and is made up of lots of different actions, some of which may seem harmless but which can prove extremely distressing to the victim.

Assignments

Brainstorming

⇨ In small groups, discuss what you know about domestic violence. Consider the following:

- What does the term 'domestic violence' mean?

- Does domestic violence encompass more than just physical violence?

- Who are the perpetrators of domestic violence?

Research

⇨ Research forced marriage in the UK. Write some notes about the key issues surrounding this topic and share with your class.

⇨ Do some research and find out about male victims of domestic violence. Make notes on some of the statistics you discover and feedback to your class.

⇨ Research Clare's Law and make notes about what the law entails and why it was given its name.

⇨ Look at the *Domestic violence legislation in England and Wales: timeline* on page 27. Do some research into domestic violence-based law in the UK and create your own timeline, adding to the points that are already there. Choose how you display your information, e.g. on a poster.

⇨ Create a questionnaire to find out how many people in your class are aware that domestic abuse can happen after a relationship has ended. Use your findings to draw a graph that illustrates the results.

⇨ Find out about rehabilitation programmes for domestic violence perpetrators. What do these entail? Do they work? Write 500 words exploring your findings.

⇨ Where does the phrase *Cathy Come Home* originate from? Do some research and feedback to your class.

Design

⇨ Choose one of the articles in this book and create an illustration to highlight the key themes/messages of your chosen piece.

⇨ Read the article *Myths vs facts* on page 4. In small groups, think about how you could raise public awareness of these myths and design a campaign based on your ideas. For example, you could storyboard a television advert, plan a social media campaign or design a series of posters and banners that could be displayed in public spaces.

⇨ Design a leaflet that could be displayed at your local vets, which offers advice for people who have pets and are concerned about what might happen to them if they were to leave their abusive partner.

⇨ Imagine you have been asked to design a leaflet that will be made available in your local GP's surgery. The leaflet should explain the key facts about domestic and relationship abuse, as well as busting some of the myths surrounding it. Include a list of resources people can go to for information and support.

Oral

⇨ With a partner, create a five-minute PowerPoint presentation that explores the issue of domestic violence in teenage relationships. You should include a section about resources such as websites and charities that young people can consult if they are experiencing these issues.

⇨ Your friend tells you that their boyfriend/girlfriend is being emotionally abusive. Role play a situation in which you ask about this behaviour and give advice.

⇨ As a class, discuss why you think male victims of domestic violence are less likely to come forward and discuss their abuse.

⇨ New laws mean that people who share explicit pictures or videos of former partners can be prosecuted. In small groups, discuss your feelings about this law and what kind of sentence you think would be appropriate under these circumstances. Share the key points of your discussion with the rest of your class.

⇨ Do you think there should be refuges available for male victims of domestic violence? Discuss with your class.

⇨ In pairs, discuss why victims choose to stay with abusive partners.

Reading/writing

⇨ Write a one-paragraph definition of domestic violence. Share your definition with a partner and discuss the differences and similarities between your ideas.

⇨ Read *What is gaslighting?* on page 6 and write a short-story that illustrates this issue.

⇨ Write a diary entry from the point of view of a parent who is suffering domestic violence at the hands of their child. Your entry should be at least 500 words long.

⇨ Write a letter to your local MP explaining why you believe the Government should ensure that domestic violence refuges are not closed.

⇨ Watch the film *Sleeping with the Enemy*, starring Julia Roberts. Write a review, focusing on the film's theme of domestic violence.

⇨ Imagine that you write an Agony Aunt/Uncle column in a popular women's magazine. A reader has written to you explaining that she thinks she might be experiencing domestic abuse from her partner. The abuse is not physical but emotional. Write a reply, advising her on what steps she can take to leave the abusive situation.

Acknowledgements

The publisher is grateful for permission to reproduce the material in this book. While every care has been taken to trace and acknowledge copyright, the publisher tenders its apology for any accidental infringement or where copyright has proved untraceable. The publisher would be pleased to come to a suitable arrangement in any such case with the rightful owner.

Images

All images courtesy of iStock, except pages 30 & 34: Pixabay and 32 © GRVO TV

Icon on pages 6 & 37 made by Freepik from www.flaticon.com

Illustrations

Don Hatcher: pages 12 & 29. Simon Kneebone: pages 11 & 37. Angelo Madrid: pages 7 & 24.

Additional acknowledgements

Editorial on behalf of Independence Educational Publishers by Cara Acred.

With thanks to the Independence team: Mary Chapman, Sandra Dennis, Christina Hughes, Jackie Staines and Jan Sunderland.

Cara Acred

Cambridge

May 2016